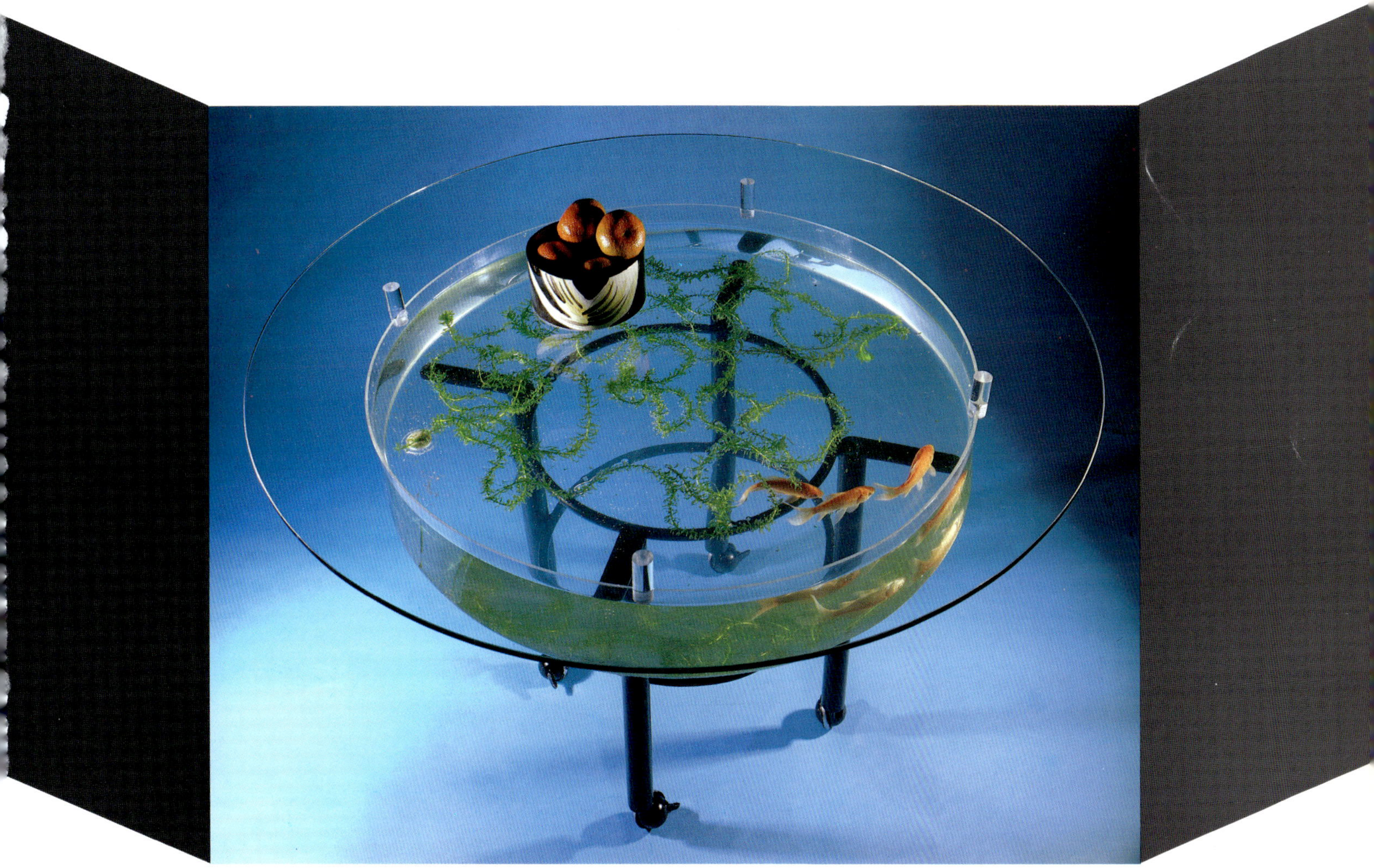

Preceding page:
1. Paula Sweet. *Table with Water and Fish*. 1981.
Glass, plastic, steel, height: 34"; diameter: 48".
Courtesy L. A. Louver Gallery, Venice, California

Opposite:
2. Kim MacConnel. *Painting, Chair, Lamp*.
Da Loop (painting). 1979. Acrylic on cotton, 8'4" ×9'10";
Chair. 1978. Found chair, paint, 45×22×22";
Sports Lamp. 1978. Plastic bowling pin, ball, golf club,
oar, metal standing ashtray, height: 60".
Collection the artist, Encinitas, California

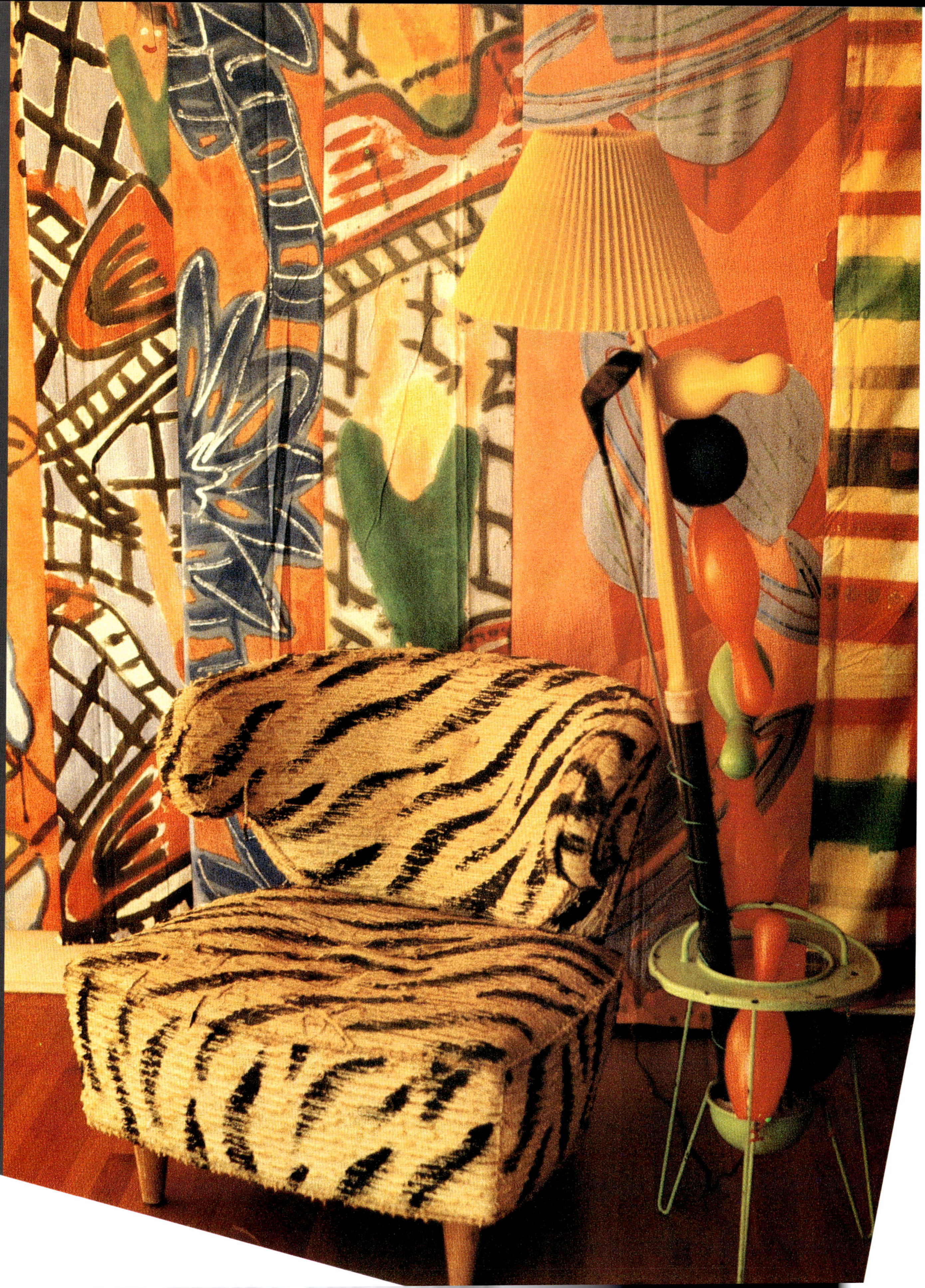

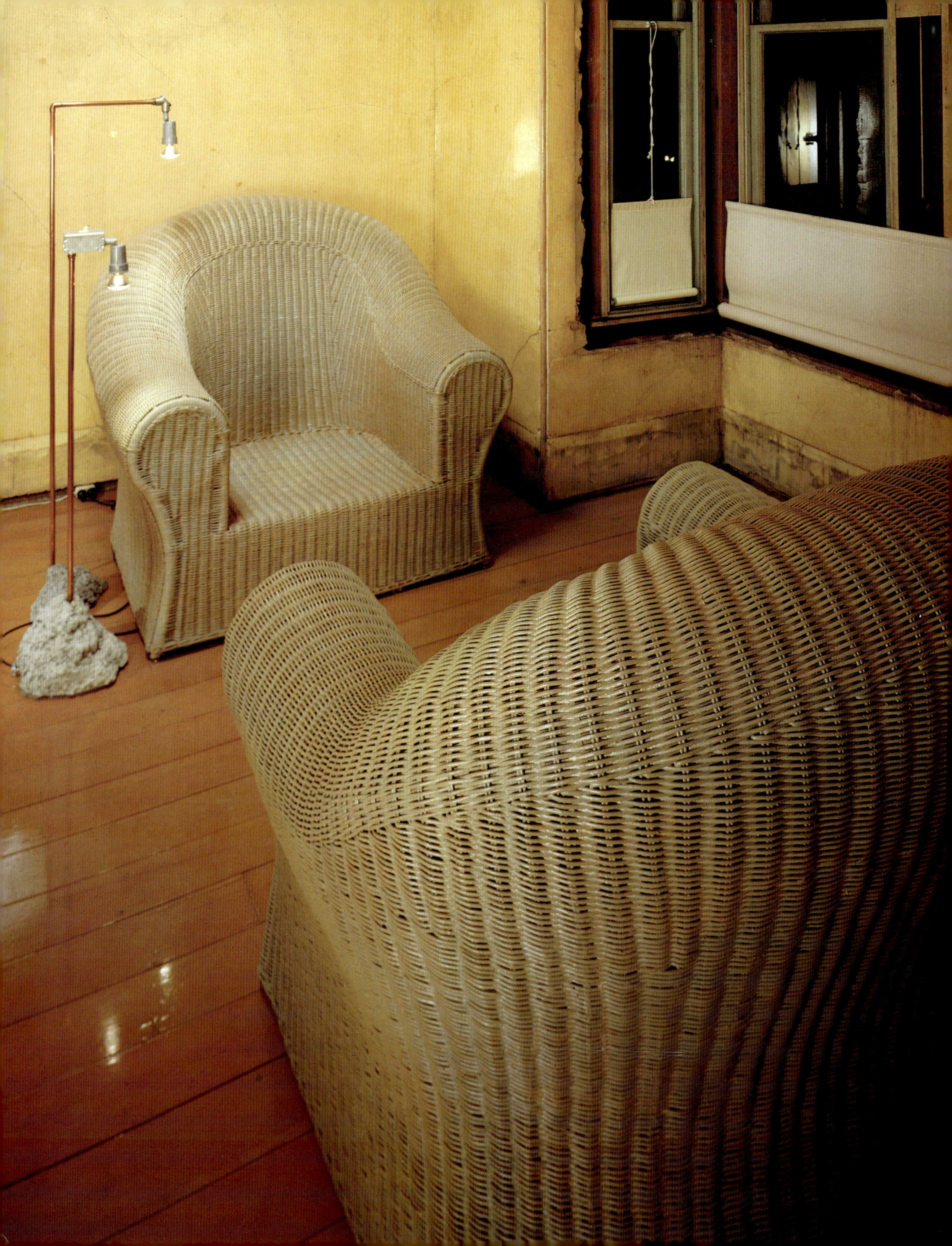

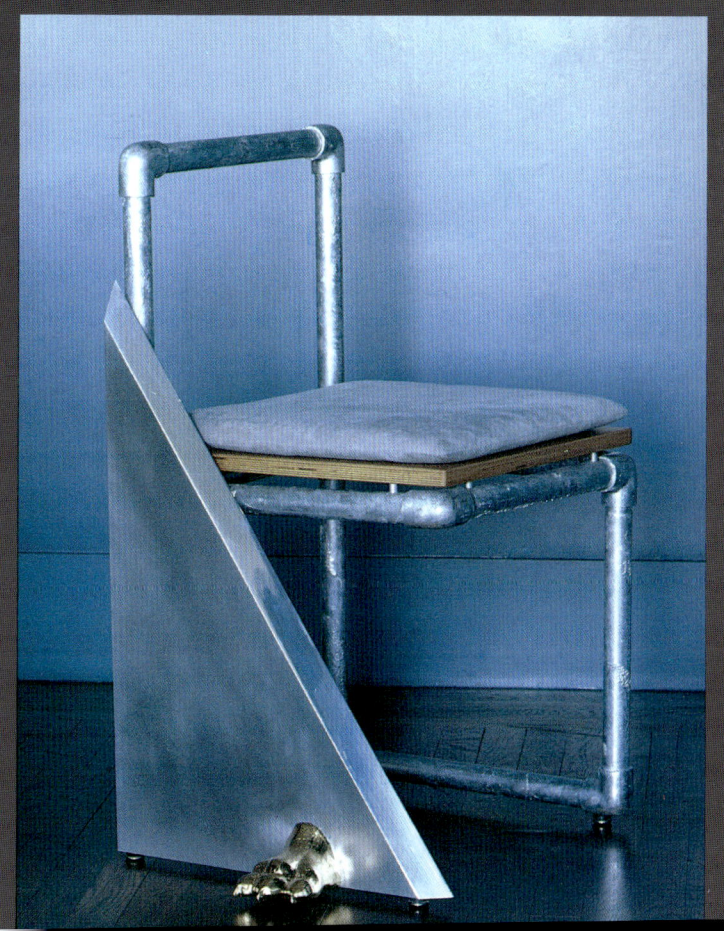

Left:
3. David Ireland.
South China Chair.
1979. Pelembang cane,
paint, 42 × 48 × 48".
Lamp. 1982.
Concrete, copper tubing,
miscellaneous electrical parts,
height: 50".
Leah Levy Gallery, San Francisco

Above, left:
4. Stephen de Staebler.
Valentine Throne. 1974.
Stoneware, low-fired clay,
42 × 33 × 30".
Courtesy Oakland Museum,
California

Above, right:
5. Alan Siegel. *Big Julie.* 1982.
Poplar, black walnut, paint,
51 × 28 × 45". Courtesy Nancy
Hoffman Gallery, New York

Right:
6. Robert Wilson. *Side Chair.* 1982.
Wood, plumbing pipe,

7. Richard Artschwager.
Table with Pink Tablecloth.
1964. Formica on wood,
25¼ × 44 × 44".
Courtesy Leo Castelli Gallery,
New York

8. Masayuki Oda.
Bench. 1982.
Concrete, wood, paint,
16 × 22 × 14".
Collection the artist,
Los Angeles

10. R. M. Fischer. *Bertha*. 1982. Boiler duct, plumbing pipe, plastic reflectors, crystal, 60 × 38 × 34". Collection the artist, New York

9. Whit Kent. *Fish Chest*. 1980. Pinewood painted, varnished, and waxed, 14 × 16 × 10". Courtesy Julie: Artisans' Gallery, New York

Below:
11. Alan Siegel. *Star Fish*. 1981. Poplar, stain, 42½ × 41 × 21". Courtesy Nancy Hoffman Gallery, New York

LE CORPS SEX IONNÉ
BB MA VIE
CALEPIN
ARE YOU CONFUSED?
BOSSUET
ERUDIMINI
Mme GUYON
THÉOLOGIE ASTRALE
VOYAGE BIBLIOGRAPHIQUE
LE GOÛT
VISIONS

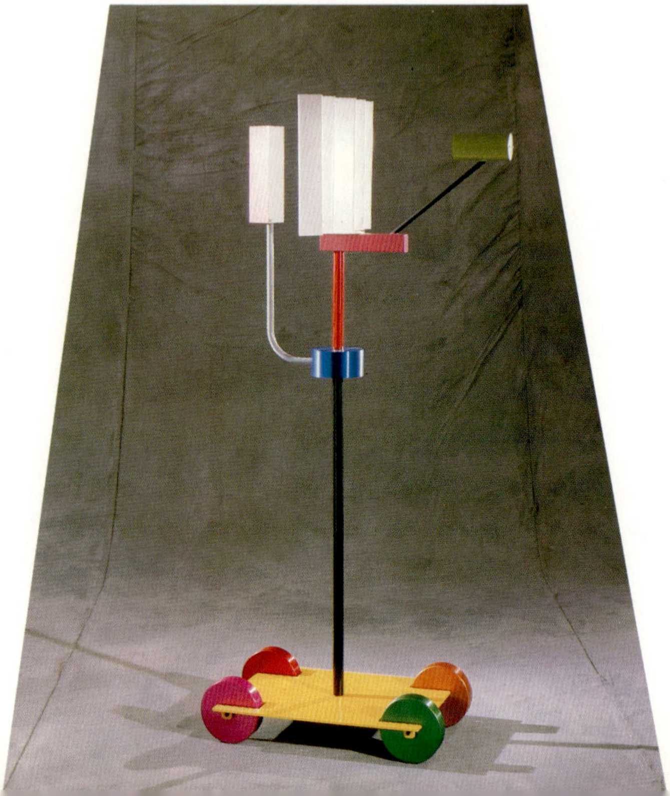

13. Guy de Cointet. Set for *De Toute les Couleurs*, Theatre du Rond-Point, Paris. 1982.
Furniture, walls, door, and window: painted wood; other props: painted cardboard.
Courtesy Yves Lefevbre Productions, Paris

Opposite, left:
14. Peter Shire.
Henry (Freestanding Shelf). 1982.
Wood, steel, lacquer, 47 × 39 × 18".
Collection Jacob and Ruth Bloom, Los Angeles

Opposite, right:
15. Peter Shire.
Corrugated Light Wheels. 1982.
Steel, anodized aluminum,
lacquer, 71 × 31 × 28".
Janus Gallery, Los Angeles

16. Leo Sewell. *Table*. 1981.
Reclaimed objects, 25 × 22 × 19".
Collection the artist, Philadelphia

17. James Hong. *Karnak*. Bookcases. 1979.
Wood, glass, lacquer, electrical, telephone, and cable outlets, 60×16".
Art et Industrie, New York

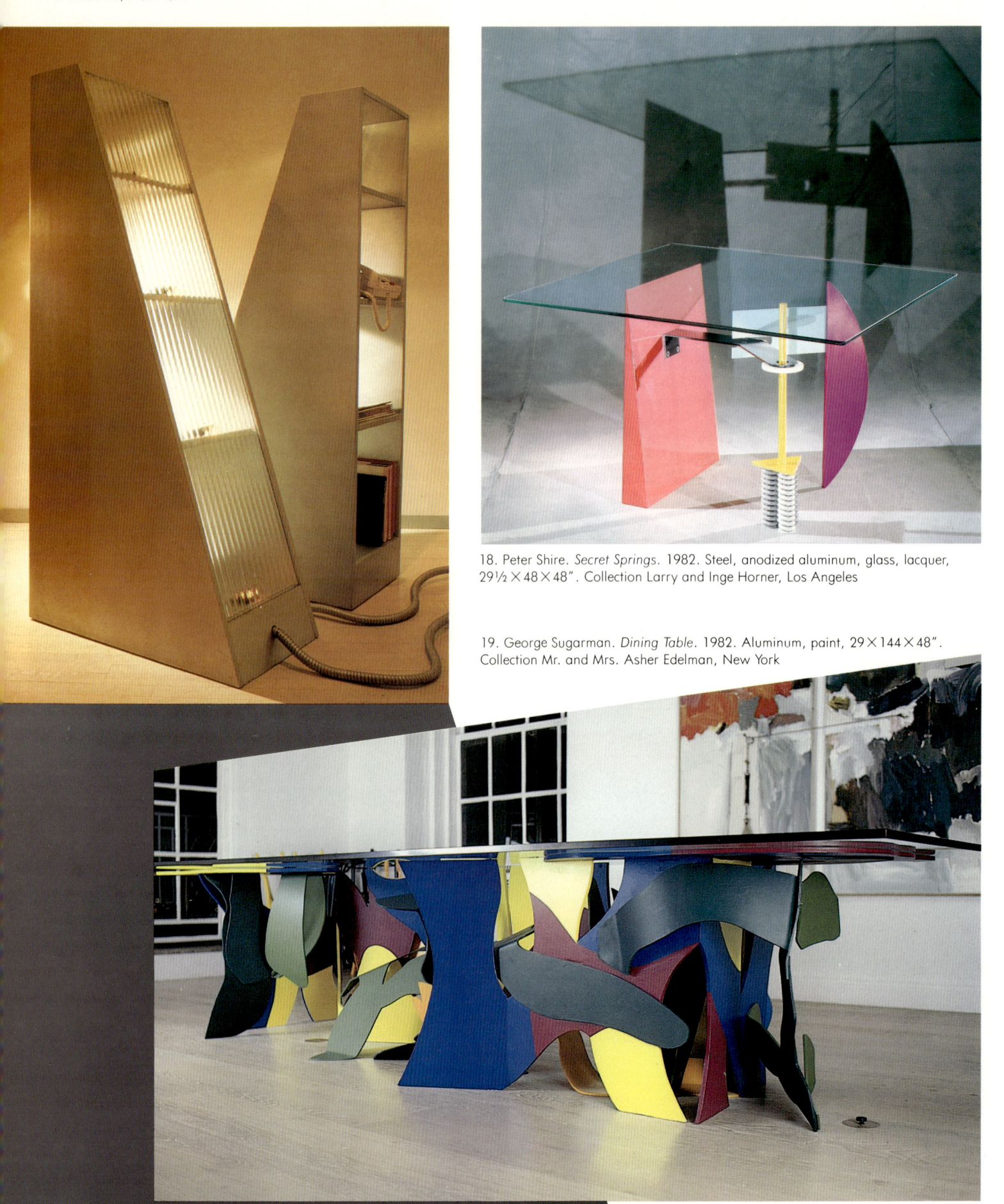

18. Peter Shire. *Secret Springs*. 1982. Steel, anodized aluminum, glass, lacquer, 29½×48×48". Collection Larry and Inge Horner, Los Angeles

19. George Sugarman. *Dining Table*. 1982. Aluminum, paint, 29×144×48". Collection Mr. and Mrs. Asher Edelman, New York

20. Larry Bell. *Furniture de Lux Living Room*. 1980–81. Carpathian elm burl, bird's-eye maple, cotton velvet, glass, aluminum, silicon monoxide. Installation includes: *Sofa de Lux II*, 33 × 88 × 35"; *Chairs I*, 32 × 26 × 32"; *Coffee Table I*, 16 × 60 × 34"; *Corner Lamps*, 36 × 36". Collection the artist, Taos, New Mexico

21. Ron Cooper and Robert Mangurian. *Wire Glass Desk*. 1980. Wire glass, silicon rubber, zolotone paint. 30 × 60 × 36"

22. Scott Burton.
Storage Cubes I. 1979–80.
Wood, lacquer, hinges,
40½ × 30 × 30".
Collection Barry Lowen,
Los Angeles

23. Kim MacConnel. *Couch, End Table, Lamp.*
Curved Pink Couch. 1982. Upholstered sofa, acrylic, 33×92×41".
Harlequin End Table. 1982. Wood table, acrylic, 31½×30×21".
Lamp. 1982. Found lamp, acrylic, 35×10".
Courtesy Alberta College of Art Gallery, Calgary, Alberta, Canada

24. Susan Linnell. *Screen, Table, Chair.* 1982. Pine, fiberglass, acrylic, screen: 53×73"; table: 29×72×42"; chair: 45×22×21". Collection the artist, Albuquerque, New Mexico

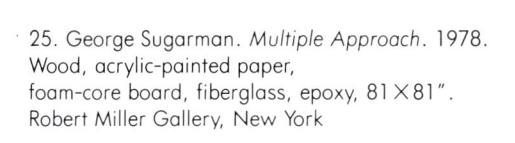

25. George Sugarman. *Multiple Approach.* 1978. Wood, acrylic-painted paper, foam-core board, fiberglass, epoxy, 81×81". Robert Miller Gallery, New York

26. Jack Youngerman.
Two Blues.
Folding screen,
front and back.
1978. Oil on linen,
72×144".
Washburn Gallery,
New York

Opposite:
27. Jack Youngerman. *Fire/Orange*. Folding screen, front and back. 1978. Oil and acrylic, raw linen, 72 × 144". Collection Cooper-Hewitt Museum, The Smithsonian Institution's National Museum of Design, New York

Right:
28. Paula Sweet. *Light Tower*. 1982. Paper with reinforced steel, height: 96"; diameter: 42". Courtesy L. A. Louver Gallery, Venice, California

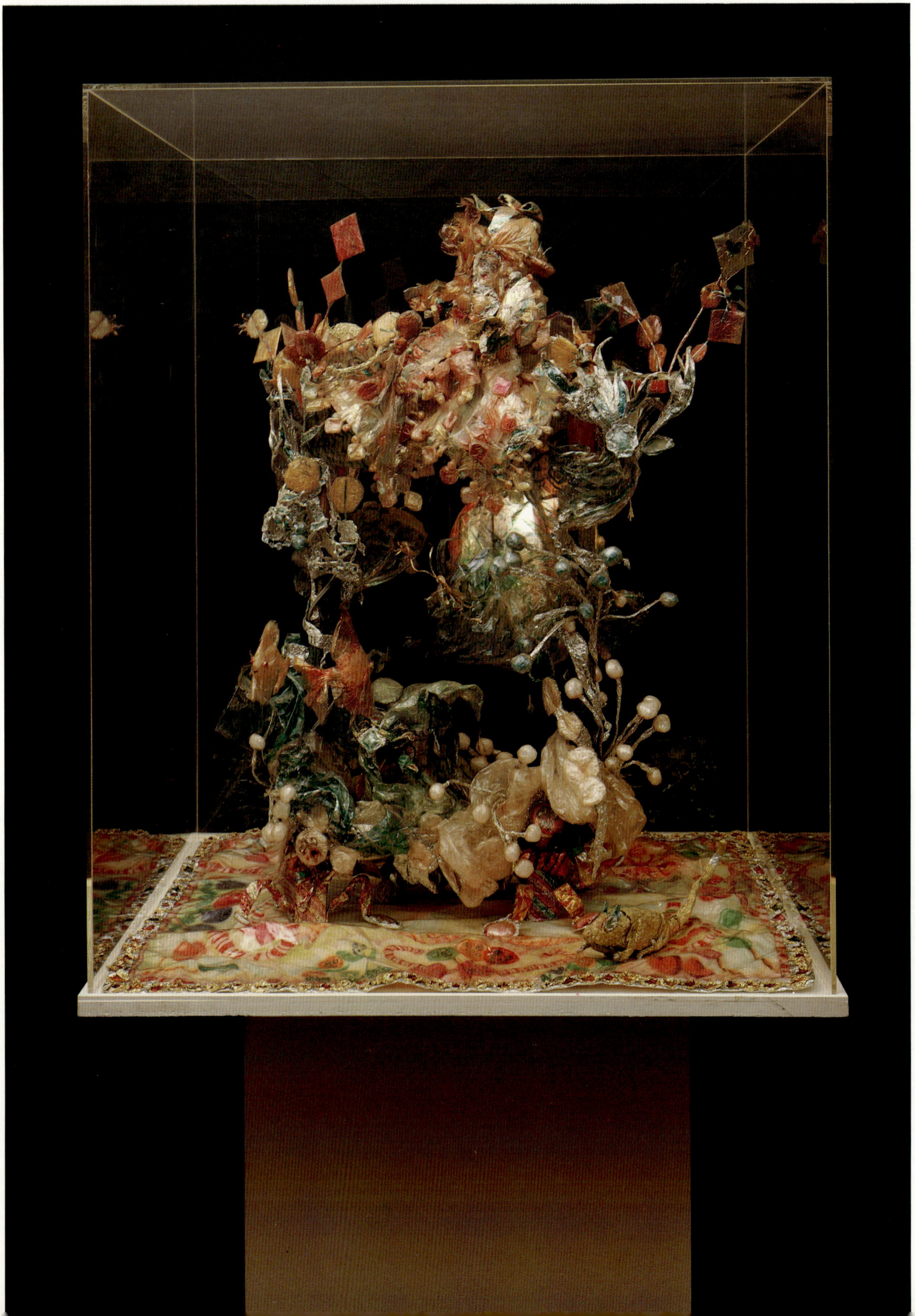

Opposite:
29. Thomas Lanigan-Schmidt.
Daytime/Nite Light (A Solitary Drinker). 1973.
Mixed media, 40½ × 24½ × 15".
Courtesy Holly Solomon Gallery, New York

Left:
30. Judy Kensley McKie.
Snake Stand. 1981.
Painted poplar, 40 × 14 × 14".
Collection Patricia Conway,
Brooklyn, New York

Pages 18–19:
31. Robert Guillot. *Untitled (Pink Chair)*. 1980.
Stainless steel tubing, vinyl, 29 × 25 × 47".
Multiples/Marian Goodman Gallery, New York

Pages 20–21:
32. John Chamberlain.
Thordis's Barge. 1980–81.
Urethane foam, fabric, 29½ × 11'6" × 12'8".
© Dia Art Foundation 1982, New York

HARRY N. ABRAMS, INC., PUBLISHERS, NEW YORK

Artists
Design
Furniture

Denise

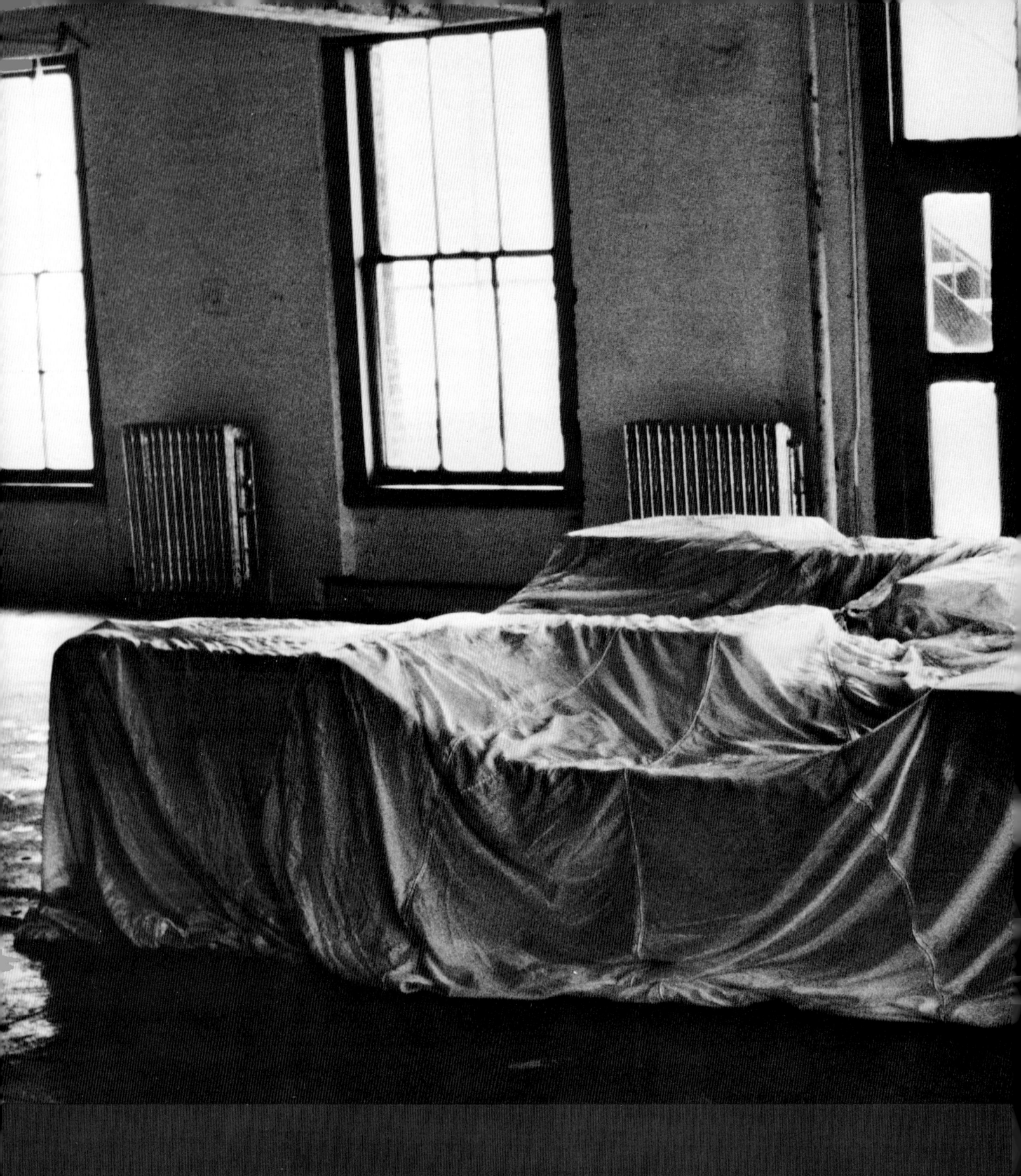

PROJECT MANAGER: LETA BOSTELMAN
EDITOR: ANNE YAROWSKY
DESIGNER: CAROL ROBSON

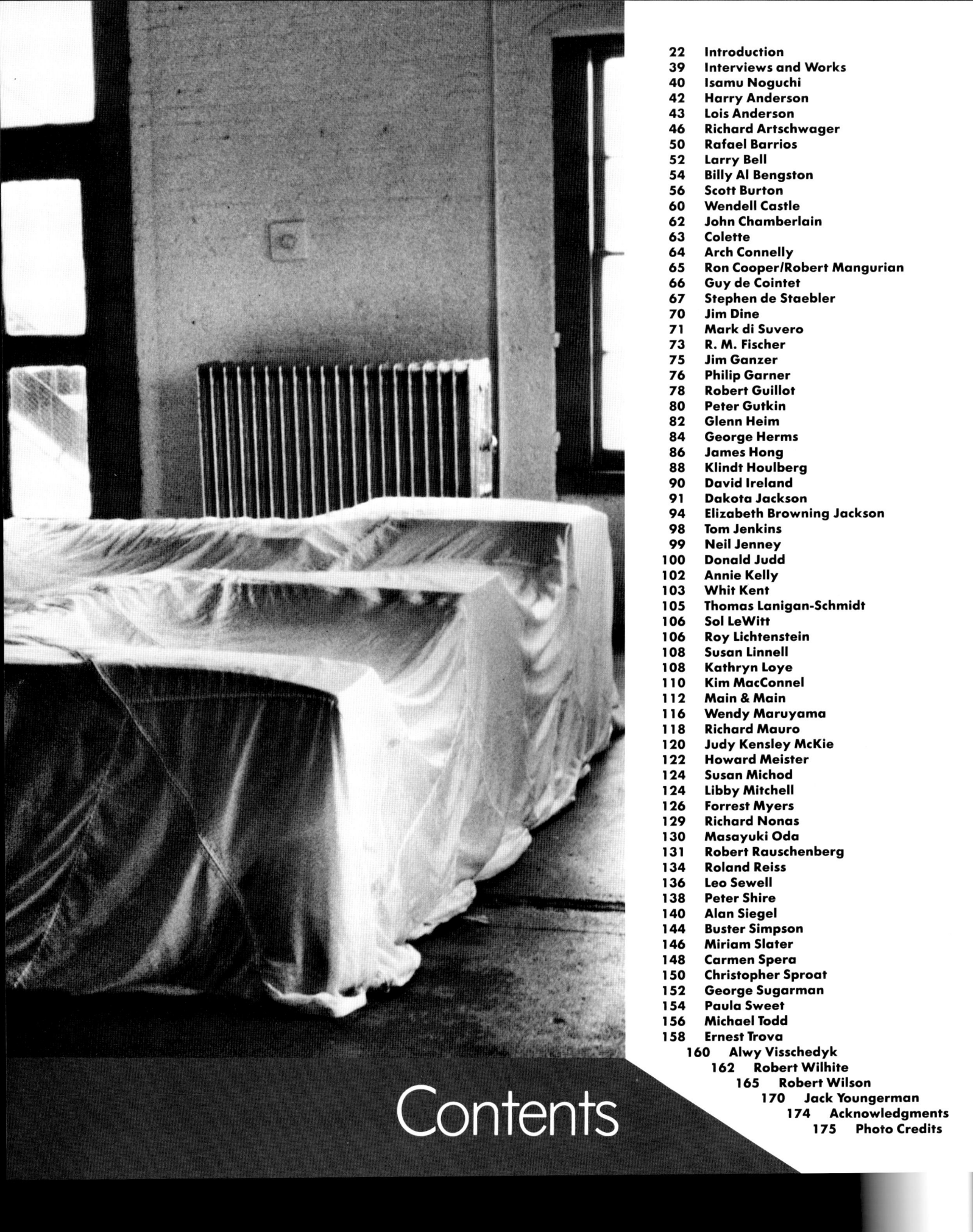

22	Introduction
39	Interviews and Works
40	Isamu Noguchi
42	Harry Anderson
43	Lois Anderson
46	Richard Artschwager
50	Rafael Barrios
52	Larry Bell
54	Billy Al Bengston
56	Scott Burton
60	Wendell Castle
62	John Chamberlain
63	Colette
64	Arch Connelly
65	Ron Cooper/Robert Mangurian
66	Guy de Cointet
67	Stephen de Staebler
70	Jim Dine
71	Mark di Suvero
73	R. M. Fischer
75	Jim Ganzer
76	Philip Garner
78	Robert Guillot
80	Peter Gutkin
82	Glenn Heim
84	George Herms
86	James Hong
88	Klindt Houlberg
90	David Ireland
91	Dakota Jackson
94	Elizabeth Browning Jackson
98	Tom Jenkins
99	Neil Jenney
100	Donald Judd
102	Annie Kelly
103	Whit Kent
105	Thomas Lanigan-Schmidt
106	Sol LeWitt
106	Roy Lichtenstein
108	Susan Linnell
108	Kathryn Loye
110	Kim MacConnel
112	Main & Main
116	Wendy Maruyama
118	Richard Mauro
120	Judy Kensley McKie
122	Howard Meister
124	Susan Michod
124	Libby Mitchell
126	Forrest Myers
129	Richard Nonas
130	Masayuki Oda
131	Robert Rauschenberg
134	Roland Reiss
136	Leo Sewell
138	Peter Shire
140	Alan Siegel
144	Buster Simpson
146	Miriam Slater
148	Carmen Spera
150	Christopher Sproat
152	George Sugarman
154	Paula Sweet
156	Michael Todd
158	Ernest Trova
160	Alwy Visschedyk
162	Robert Wilhite
165	Robert Wilson
170	Jack Youngerman
174	Acknowledgments
175	Photo Credits

Contents

33. Claes Oldenburg. *Room* (detail). 1964. Courtesy Sidney Janis Gallery, New York

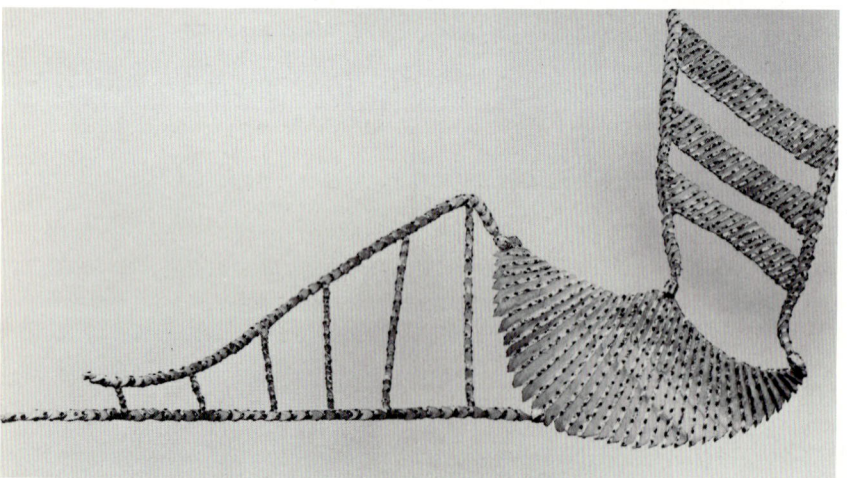

35. Lucas Samaras. *Chair Transformation #12, 1969*. 1969–70. Acrylic and wood, 40 × 36 × 12". Courtesy The Pace Gallery, New York

34. Margaret Wharton. *Odalisque*. 1980. Wood, chair, epoxy, vinyl wallpaper samples, black glitter, 51½ × 99½ × 2". Courtesy Phyllis Kind Gallery, New York

Introduction

> There is bound to be some common ground between layman and artist, where a mutual approach is possible and whence the artist no longer appears as a being totally apart.
>
> —Paul Klee, 1924

Around 1980 I began to notice that in my circle of acquaintances alone there were artists doing astonishing things in an area tangential to their art. Poking around studios and living spaces, I ran across pieces of furniture the likes of which I had never seen before, and this furniture had all been made by the artists themselves. Furthermore I found that there was little communication among the artists about this seemingly clandestine sideline in which they were engaged. Rarely had any of the artists seen each other's furniture, and there was absolutely no evidence of an exchange of ideas. Rather, each artist had a very personal source of inspiration for his pieces, and most often these pieces filled a strictly personal need. The degree and randomness of invention piqued my curiosity. I pursued my investigation wherever I happened to find myself and was surprised and encouraged by the array of work I smoked out in cities with concentrated communities of artists. I found that this activity was actually widespread, yet lacked the earmarks of a movement per se. It was a completely heterogeneous proliferation of ideas that seemed to redefine the structures of everyday life.

In pursuing my research I was increasingly confounded by the body of furniture-related, nonfunctional art. This work used the furniture form as its point of departure or incorporated it as an important symbolic element. I came upon well-known artists such as Claes Oldenburg, Lucas Samaras, Ed Kienholz, Margaret Wharton, Robert Morris, Barbara Zucker, Bruce Conner, Vito Acconci, and Joel Shapiro, all of whom altered scale and materials, transformed, distorted, disassembled, simplified, and abstracted the form.

Despite the appeal of this work, however, I forced myself to compress my focus further and harness the temptation to include nonfunctional furniture. I gambled on the hunch that artists consciously or unconsciously draw from the same formal and philosophical legacy, a legacy that would be reflected in the strictly functional furniture they created.

Another body of material I encountered did not make can crafts tradition. In the last twenty years American craftsmen have transformed crafts furniture from the native, homespun art it once was. They have manipulated their materials with a technical virtuosity and freedom that is impressive and moving, and have invented forms that are truly challenging.

As one would expect, their work was better crafted in many cases than was the furniture made by artists. Though their backgrounds and approaches to the subject are different, the work stands on its own. I had to draw the line or be overwhelmed. What interested me for the time being were the conceptual crossovers that fine artists make when they tackle a specific area of object making.

Virtually from the outset, therefore, I established a strict set of parameters for selecting the furniture to be included in this book: (1) the furniture-maker had to be grounded in the "fine art" tradition; (2) the furniture had to be intended for use in the home to some degree; (3) considerable thought must have been given to it, wherever it fell on the spectrum between pure art and expedient utility and; (4) I would have to select a representative sampling that expressed the variety of points of view and visual richness of the total body of material. But the temptation to include what lay tantalizingly just outside the predefined scope of the project gnawed at the edges of my resolve just the same and a few borderline concessions were made.

At the time I began my research, media attention was infrequent on the subject of artists' furniture, but as I went on with the project, there seemed to be a concurrent swell of interest, with articles in magazines and newspapers exposing this type of work to the general public. There was an increasing number of exhibitions under the aegis of art galleries, museums, design centers, and alternative spaces. For the most part, however, this furniture was the kind of work that was rarely exhibited due to its position somewhere in the gap between fine art and utilitarian object. Typically it was a one-of-a-kind exercise that remained confined to the artist's studio or to a private home or office once a commission was completed.

36. Edward Kienholz. *The Wait.* 1964–65. Tableau: epoxy, glass, wood, and found objects, 80 × 148 × 78".
Collection of The Whitney Museum of American Art, New York.
Gift of the Howard and Jean Lipman Foundation, Inc.

37. Bruce Conner. *Couch.* 1963.
Assemblage, mixed media, 32 × 70¾ × 27".
Norton Simon Museum of Art at Pasadena, California.
Purchased with funds donated by Mr. David H. Steinmetz III

38. Robert Morris. *The Hearing*. 1972. Mixed media. Courtesy Leo Castelli Gallery, New York

39. Joel Shapiro. *Untitled*. 1973-74. Cast Iron, 3 × 1¼ × 1¼". Collection Giuseppe Panza di Biumo

In the United States, critical attempts at situating artists' furniture on the modern art continuum have been tentative and ambiguous. The confusion appears to arise out of the unorthodox hybridization of two mutually exclusive domains in our culture: "functional furniture" and "art." Traditionally, art has been held apart from the banalities of life as a kind of separate plane of human achievement, and furniture has been accorded a secondary position in the hierarchy of aesthetic values. To allow that function and art could abide together in one work borders on apostasy to some in the art world.

In a country like Japan, however, the distinction is moot. There functionality does not preclude art. Art can be expressed in all spheres of human endeavor. The expression of art can be found in utilitarian objects, and that expression is in no way inferior. The most profound resonances can emanate from a lowly object as well as from an aristocratic, rare, or purely contemplative one. It need not have the patina of age to elicit awe. When a craftsman truly loses himself in his craft, his hands become those of nature and the beauty of creative essence emerges. That quality can manifest itself anywhere, can permeate any aspect of human life. That intimate alignment and fusion of the artist or artisan with the spirit of nature inhabits the piece and gives it life and continuing significance to viewers whose traditions, rooted in Zen, have honed their perceptions.

In Africa, a chieftain's stool is at once a finely crafted ritual object denoting rank and expressing an animistic belief system and an item of daily use.

And so it is with most non-Western cultures. Utilitarian objects are endowed with symbolism and beauty, and life and art are integrated. But in the United States a dichotomy exists between the two. Art since the 1940s has become increasingly isolated from the mainstream of everyday life. In assuming the lead in modern art, the United States chose a course that emphasized stratification of artistic activity over consolidation of the revolutionary ferment of integration that had taken place earlier in the century.

It was then that artists and architects all over Europe responded to a new set of moral imperatives brought on by World War I and social and aesthetic upheavals. These events profoundly affected the fundamental definitions, sources, and goals of art and architecture in the West. A rapidly spiraling polemic surrounding the role of art in everyday life began to build on itself, and gradually the principles raised brought art and furniture as close to integration as they have ever come in our culture.

The first stirrings of radical change, however, occurred late in the nineteenth century, when artists and architects began to sense the pressures of a new technology crying out for exploitation on its own terms. This period witnessed the flowering of the industrial age and the rise of a huge urban middle class. Art lagged behind in the climate of change. Mired in effete romanticism, it served up sentiment in line with the prescriptions of the academies to a complacent bourgeoisie. Design and architecture, too,

40. *Pende* (Gungu region, Congo-Kinshasa). Chief's chair, influenced by European design. Wood and leather, height 38¼". Museum Rietberg, Zurich

41. Pablo Picasso. *Les Demoiselles d'Avignon.* 1907. Oil on canvas, 96 × 92". Collection, The Museum of Modern Art, New York. Acquired through the Lillie P. Bliss Bequest

42. Georges Braque. *Musical Forms (Guitar and Clarinet).* 1918. Pasted paper, corrugated cardboard, charcoal and gouache on cardboard, 30⅜ × 37⅜". Philadelphia Museum of Art. The Louise and Walter Arensberg Collection

Opposite:

harkened to the past for stylistic references. The new materials of industry were used to elaborate a sentimental eclecticism rather than give birth to the new forms latent in the technology.

An early attempt at reviving ideals corrupted by the materialistic, redundant values of the industrial age was the Arts and Crafts movement in England in the late nineteenth century. Its founder, William Morris, believed that the machine dehumanized design and robbed it of aesthetic merit. Morris called for a return to the cultural integration of the Middle Ages, when art, politics, morality, and religion all formed one living whole. He associated himself with fine artists in his undertaking. Though he pioneered an early fusion of fine art and applied art and advocated formal principles of mass, line, and color in the decorative arts, his were nostalgic efforts only a select few could afford. He was fundamentally romantic and refused to respond to his time; thus his impact remained limited. However, just before the turn of the century in America, the architects Louis Sullivan and Frank Lloyd Wright met the challenge of the age as a social mandate and succeeded in breaking conclusively with the past. Sullivan's modernist creed "Form follows function" and Frank Lloyd Wright's use of volume and mass and his attention to the whole environment, including its furnishings, came to exert an enormous impact on the development of ideas in the architecture and design movements of the twentieth century, particularly the Bauhaus in Germany and De Stijl in Holland.

Paris at the end of the nineteenth century was a cosmopolitan hub of artistic activity. The stylistic innovations of some of its painters provided a forward momentum, generated, for example, by Van Gogh's expressive handling of paint, Seurat's Pointillism, and Gaugin's decorative patterns. Most of all Cézanne's structured and ambiguous space presaged the overthrow of the old order. But these innovations were still essentially conservative. It was Cubism at the beginning of the twentieth century that mounted the first frontal attack on academic tradition. In one lightning blow it stripped the academy of its position as aesthetic arbiter and reformulated the visual lexicon of art and architecture for the twentieth century.

With their brilliant blend of Cézannean principles and primitive art, Picasso and Braque are credited with delivering up to the world, in 1907 and 1908, its first "modern" paintings. From that point on ineffable truths would no longer be expressed via anecdotal imitation of nature, which was now the realm of photography, but through pure color, mathematical logic, geometric lines and planes, and volumetric units. The force of this breakthrough stimulated an abundance of new visual theories throughout pre-World War I Europe, some of which were Futurism, Orphism, and Constructivism. Geometry became the emotional equivalent of Nature, and this idea launched a formal approach to art, architecture, and design that would carry to the present.

Around 1912 Cubism introduced another important innovation: collage. What Braque initiated, Picasso, the tireless experimenter, pushed to the limits. The illusion of dimension no longer relied on the representational depiction of it. The addition of typography from newspapers, cardboard, sand, metal, and other waste materials of everyday life called attention to the reality of the surface. This new conception of the picture plane, constructed literally of odd materials in relief, gave birth to the genres of assemblage and sculptural construction and emulsified the formerly incompatible disciplines of sculpture and painting. These bold techniques were later enlarged by the Dadaists and Surrealists, and by Picasso himself.

Picasso was a passionate renegade whose Promethean artistic output spanned over half the century. His selection of common objects and industrial discards in his sculptures and reliefs contributed to their acceptance as materials in art. No territory was off limits. In 1910 he designed upholstery for Gertrude Stein's chairs, and in the forties he began a staggering production of utilitarian ceramic objects.

At about the same time, the peasant-born Rumanian sculptor Constantin Brancusi was developing the new abstraction from his own source of inspiration: the myths, symbols, and forms of Rumanian folk art. A calm, detached figure, he warily kept his distance from the artistic commotion of Cubism and sought "the essence of things" on his own. He had a mystical sense of the universality of life, and his quieter geometry derived from nature. Simplicity and self-sufficiency were deeply ingrained in him. He relied on himself for everything, even mending his own broken leg. It was crucial that he create his own integrated world in order "to get into the mood to do things." His first years of apprenticeship with a cabinetmaker in Rumania served him well. His rough-hewn stools, benches, wooden seats, and bed evoked a peasant interior with its wooden pillars and gave him the serenity he required in his quest for "ultimate truth."

Meanwhile Cubism was spreading quickly beyond the entourage of Picasso and Braque to Europe and the United States, and by the eve of World War I it was *the* avant-garde style of the day. Art took on the seriousness of scientific theory, and true to the law that for every action there is an opposite and equal reaction, Dadaism sprang up.

At the outbreak of World War I abstract theorizing was temporarily shelved. Everyone went to war. Creative refugees in the neutral zones took advantage of their freedom and gave vent to their tension, skepticism, loss of idealism, and sense of absurdity and meaninglessness by revolting against art itself. In the midst of profound chaos, disintegration, and uncertainty, they rebelled against the constraints of this budding intellectual orthodoxy.

Zurich during the war was a haven for "a few independent spirits who live for other ideals." In 1916 Hugo Ball founded the notorious Cabaret Voltaire, an arena for iconoclasm that verged unabashedly on nonsense. Unlike Cubism and related "isms" that sought to justify themselves, Dada declared itself, in Ball's words, "foolery extracted from the emptiness in which all the higher problems are wrapped, a gladiator's gesture, a game played with the shabby remnants . . . a public execution of false morality."

In 1915, in New York, Marcel Duchamp, with his friends Picabia and Man Ray, similarly challenged art's frame of reference and broke new ground. They declared that conventional "retinal" art was dead. Theirs was not a pessimistic nihilism, but one suffused with ironic and playful humor. They felt that the final destruction of all values would free a hackneyed humanity and that out of the void, unpredictable, irrepressible life would bubble up to refresh and renew it. They preferred spontaneity to the stifling ethics of the spirit, expression over conscious creativity, continuous revolutions over final resolutions. Dada art became a cerebral game, an agile, puckish state of mind.

Duchamp at this time had already given up the conventional forms of painting and sculpture and made his first "Readymade," a bicycle wheel attached to a kitchen stool. He stated: "A point that I want very much to establish is that the choice of these Readymades was never dictated by aesthetic delectation; the choice was based on a reaction of visual indifference with a total absence of good or bad taste . . . in fact, a complete anesthesia." The shameless effrontery of Duchamp's Readymades effectively made their point. Foreshadowing the Surrealist "total revolution of the object," ordinary objects or their simple displacement from the usual context allowed new and surprising levels of meaning to emerge. They also suggested that there is no difference between artist and layman and that no one need be alienated from independent, artistic expression. They invalidated the artist as one who imposes his own doctrinaire version of reality.

Duchamp pledged allegiance to mercurial chance and contradiction. Inconsistency became a way of life for him. He said: "Not to be engaged in any groove is very important for me. I want to be free, and I want to be free for myself, foremost." Duchamp's stance as a life attitude would be emulated by future generations of artists who would rebel against the pressures to fit into a formalist "groove" and follow their individual impulses.

The Dadaists accomplished the demolition of old values, but even hard-liners felt the need, after the war, to modify their nihilism. But from where would renewal spring? Everyone had read Freud and his mappings of the unconscious. Here in dreams, myths, and metaphors lay the fallow field of invention, an ever-changing, ever-ambiguous, self-renewing territory. Here lay an area pure and untainted by political deception and as real as material reality itself. The betterment of man would be achieved through total, uncommitted liberty and in detachment from things mundane. By 1924 Dadaism had evolved naturally into Surrealism with André Breton as its spokesman and the unconscious as its oracle. Thus Breton predicted: "The distinction between art and life, so long held to be necessary, will be contested and will conclude with its being canceled out in principle." To Surrealism, life itself was

44. Pablo Picasso. *Still Life*. 1914.
Painted wood with upholstery fringe,
height 10"; width 18⅞".
Lent by trustees of the Tate Gallery,
London

45. Marcel Duchamp. *Bicycle Wheel*. 1913.
Readymade aid, height 49¾".
Private collection

46. *Picasso-Toklas-Stein Chairs*.
Upholstery designed by Picasso c. 1910.
Collection of American Literature,
The Beinecke Rare Book and Manuscript Library,
Yale University

47. Constantin Brancusi.

48. Salvador Dali. *Mae West's Lips Sofa*. 1936.
Cover, shocking pink satin, 35 × 90 × 30".
The Edward James Foundation.
On loan to the Victoria and Albert Museum, London

49. Kurt Seligmann.
Ultrameuble. 1938.
Destroyed.
Courtesy Arlette Seligmann

50. Salvador Dali.
Venus de Milo with Drawers. 1936.
© SPADEM, Paris//VAGA, New York, 1983

art. The Surrealist became an explorer of the unconscious, seeking the subterranean essence of life. Personal, idiosyncratic, irrational, anarchic, sometimes narcissistic, often mystifying, art gained its raison d'être.

André Breton suggested that "objects seen in dreams should be manufactured and put into circulation" in the hope that "the multiplication of such objects of often dubiously accepted 'usefulness'" would be replaced by dream-engendered objects, "a prerequisite for the unleashing of the 'powers of invention.'"

Around 1930 the Surrealist Salvador Dali created what he called "Objects of Symbolic Function." Unlike Duchamp's prototypical but coolly intellectual Readymades, the Surrealist objects of artists like Dali were specifically chosen for their poetic content. They were essentially three-dimensional collages or constructions of accumulated, "found" articles that the Surrealists transformed or desecrated. Furniture, things that could be sat on or contain something unseen—like chairs, boxes, and chests of drawers—were rife with connotations and possibilities of poetical metamorphosis. Their anthropomorphic, feminine, exotic, sexual, mysterious, interactive character embodied well the Surrealist fetishes and dreams.

The Surrealist object was especially popular in the thirties, and some of the more notable examples of furniture made during that time were Dali's *Venus de Milo of Drawers* of 1936 and his settee in the form of Mae West's lips, realized by his friend Jean-Michel Frank; Matta's *Magritta*, made especially for Magritte in 1937; and Kurt Seligmann's 1938 *Ultrameuble*. These pieces contained all the irreverent associations and dissociations typical of the Surrealist object. The popularity of the Surrealists' invention spread to the United States via the 1936 exhibition "Fantastic Art, Dada, Surrealism" at New York's Museum of Modern Art. Though it caused a public disturbance, this exhibition had a great impact on American artists.

In 1929 the sculptor Giacometti became a member of the Surrealists, contributed writings, and participated in group exhibitions. His dream sculptures were regarded as objects by the Surrealists even though they were not composed of the usual prosaic articles. His furniture designs, however, were something else, strictly a means of support to free him from the pressures of having to sell his art. Beginning in 1930 he designed pieces for the gifted Paris interior decorator Jean-Michel Frank. His designs for standard lamps, wall sconces, chandeliers, bas-reliefs, plaster vases, and fire dogs were reminiscent of the sculpture he was making during that period, but they resembled more the worn and corroded artifacts and architectural fragments of Roman excavations: bronze lamps adorned with female heads, female hands holding torches, fluted columns, white plaster masks with empty eyes.

Another independent soul in the Surrealist circle of the twenties and thirties was Sonia Delaunay. She worked along similar lines as her husband, Robert; he was the theorist and she was the intuitive creative force. Together they

51. Sonia Delaunay wearing dress of her own design. 1925. Courtesy Albright-Knox Art Gallery, Buffalo, New York. By arrangement with AGADP, Paris

circles and Cubistic rhythms, he through painting, and she primarily through the applied arts. "There was no hiatus for me between my painting and my so-called 'decorative' works," she said, " and the 'minor genre' had never been an artistic frustration but a free expansion, a new concept of space, an application of the same research." In 1913 she made her first simultaneous dresses. Indeed, nothing was too lowly an object for her "simultaneously contrasting" color experiments, and this linked her to the Dadaists and Surrealists.

Delaunay transformed everything in her environment: cushion covers, lampshades, goblets, curtains, and quilts. She designed costumes for Diaghilev's ballet, books and posters, and many pieces of furniture. Her "poetry fashion" of the twenties predated Breton's thirties idea of the "Poem-object" where poetry interwoven with real objects caused the viewer " to speculate on their power of reciprocal exaltation." Her art covered every surface in the home and descended into the streets, escaping entrapment "between the four edges of a painting." She wanted her art to be democratic because she believed that the power of art could free every individual.

Delaunay was also considered quite "à la mode" in Paris, where the 1925 International Exhibition of Modern Decorative and Industrial Arts gave the name "Art Deco" to a style created primarily by painters, sculptors, and architects who blended Cubism, Futurism, Fauvism, and African and Egyptian styles in luxurious, unique designs for an exclusive clientele. The artists employed skilled craftsmen to execute their designs in exotic and rare materials. Beauty for its own sake rather than an ideally aesthetic functionalism was their goal, however. The Art Deco movement managed to restore, after World War I, France's cherished position as patrician leader of refinement in fashion and the decorative arts. In spite of her popularity among the fashion-conscious and her association with Dadaists and Surrealists, Sonia Delaunay's core of idealism allied her in spirit with the more socially minded art and design movements of post-World War I Europe.

The reality of World War I had interjected itself starkly into the consciences of the more pragmatic stream of artistic thought in a different way throughout the rest of the continent. The world itself lay in physical and spiritual shambles and as many artists saw it, their work lay manifestly in rebuilding it. The enormity of the task transcended the individual approach.

The Russians had already embarked on their own very nationalistic building process, and theirs would have a great effect on the tack that Europe would take. Deeply committed to their new order, the work of the Russian avant-garde before and just after the revolution of 1917 had as its goal the establishment of a creative movement that would cut across economic and political lines and forge a brand new popular art. They would consciously synthesize European abstraction and the new materials of the industrial age. They received unprecedented, if transitory, sanction from the postrevolutionary government.

52. Kasimir Malevich. *Suprematist Composition: Airplane Flying.* 1914. Oil on canvas, 22⅞ × 19″. Collection, The Museum of Modern Art, New York

53. Sonia Delaunay. Sycamore commode. 1924

From a churning sea of Cubist-related theories, two camps emerged: the Suprematists, led by Kasimir Malevich, who developed a rational theory of pure painting based on geometric shapes, and the Constructivists, led by Vladimir Tatlin, who experimented passionately with abstract assemblages of industrial materials. He believed that each material was suggestive of form in and of itself. His most famous work was the ambitious and radical model for the "Monument to the Third International." It was a revolving building that would stand twice as high as the Empire State Building and be a landmark "union of purely artistic forms (painting, sculpture, and architecture) for a utilitarian purpose."

In the 1920s, Productivism became the utopian common ground where Suprematists and Constructivists worked together in adapting their respective theories to utilitarian ends. In a few short years there was an abundant output of films, book designs, architectural models, utilitarian objects, and furniture. El Lissitzky, a follower of Malevich best known for his hanging Suprematist constructions (Prouns), applied his theories to a wide variety of utilitarian ends, among them architecture, environmental design, and furniture. Tatlin designed a bentwood chair based on his aerodynamic experiments in wood for "flying machines." Rodchenko, another Constructivist, designed many pieces of furniture. His environment for the "Workers' Club," which included chairs, reading desks, and lamps, was exhibited in the 1925 Paris Exposition. The participation of the Russian avant-garde in this exhibition exposed all who attended to the scope of their activities.

Though under Stalin the Russian avant-garde was forced to disband and subscribe to the new official style, Social Realism, its activities from the early teens to 1930 represent the first really modernist application of art to all areas of life. Brief though it was, this period remains a powerful testament to the wealth of ideas such a practical fusion can engender.

In Holland in 1917, the painters Van Doesburg and Mondrian, the sculptor Vantongerloo, the designer Rietveld, the architects Oud and Van't Hoff, and others collaborated in the De Stijl movement to undertake "the correct task" of their time: to infuse far-ranging aspects of life with a higher sense of aesthetics, thereby bringing its polarities into equilibrium and harmony through the collective expression of style. Modern technology was enlisted as an essential tool in creating an "up-to-date" aesthetic based on the strivings in art for clarity, purity, and truth. De Stijl restricted itself to the horizontal and vertical line and to the three primary colors along with the noncolors white, black, and gray. "Above all else, truth, function, and construction are expressed," they declared. The members of De Stijl addressed themselves to the "complete expression of all our physico-spiritual demands, or, in short, the full expression of our life. [De Stijl] comprises all problems of detail, construction, creativity, and economics."

Furniture was an important component in this total harmony. Gerrit Rietveld's furniture notably bridged the

54. El Lissitzky. *Armchair.*
1930. Plexiglas.
Manufacturer: Tecta

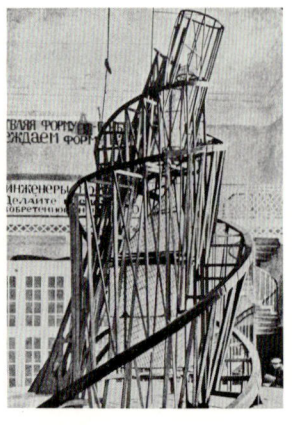

55. Vladimir Tatlin. Model for a Monument to the Third International, Moscow. 1919–20. Wood, iron, glass. Russian State Museum, Leningrad

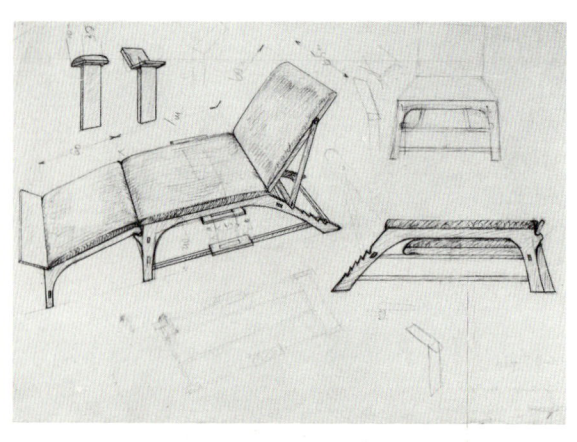

56. Aleksandr Rodchenko. Chaise lounge made for the play *Il YA.* 1929. Courtesy Centre Georges Pompidou, Paris

57. Aleksandr Rodchenko. Workers' Club presentation, l'Exposition des Arts Décoratifs, Paris. 1925. Courtesy Centre Georges Pompidou, Paris

58. Gerrit Rietveld. *Armchair.* 1917. Painted wood, height 34½". Collection, The Museum of Modern Art, New York. Gift of Philip Johnson

gap between the European developments in sculpture and painting and De Stijl's principles of harmonic design. His hope was that the chairs of De Stijl would "become the abstract, real artifacts of future interiors." Rietveld's best-known works—his Mondrianesque *Red and Blue Chair* of 1918 and his austerely sculptural *Zig-Zag Chair* of 1934, which was mass produced—have inspired many of the American artists encountered in this project, and in some cases replicas of these chairs inhabit their spaces as everyday sources of inspiration.

In Germany the future lay in mechanization and industry, and in 1919 the architect Walter Gropius founded the Bauhaus to help consolidate the artist's aesthetic ideas and the need to understand the basics of technology and design. Gropius's stated purpose was to "coordinate all creative effort, to achieve, in a new architecture, the unification of all training in art and design. The ultimate if distant goal of the Bauhaus is the *collective work of art.*"

Besides Gropius, the instructors included the painters Klee, Grosz, and Albers, former Constructivists Kandinsky and Moholy-Nagy, and the architects Marcel Breuer and Mies van der Rohe. The curriculum included the abstract theories of art and the principles of the relationship between tool and material. In the workshops the teachers encouraged "undisturbed, uninfluenced, and unprejudiced experiment" directly with the materials to allow fresh design ideas to emerge that exploited their physical properties to their best advantage.

The contribution of the Bauhaus principles to the upgrading of modern design criteria is staggering and ubiquitous, from skyscrapers to streamlined, built-in kitchens to distinctive household objects. The Bauhaus was the prime mover in the qualitative and quantitative transformation of the total environment through its successful synthesis of art, design, and its profound grasp of the potential inherent in modern technology and materials. It can be said that modern furniture design ever since the Bauhaus has been clearly directed by the forms that came out of it. Though many of its designs have been copied exactly, recent design solutions are hard pressed to match the felicitous harmony, directness, and purity of form of the classic chairs by Breuer or Mies van der Rohe. There was no artist interviewed who did not acknowledge a debt or deep admiration for its far-reaching accomplishments.

The rise of Hitler brought the dissolution of the Bauhaus in 1933. Since that time the vital and intimate alliance of artist, sculptor, architect, designer, and craftsman working together toward a common goal has never existed again. Many of the Bauhaus teachers emigrated afterward to the United States and were reassigned to specific disciplines in the American educational system, although the methods of their teaching and their activities continued to influence them all.

With the influx of Bauhaus members and Surrealists in the thirties and forties, the United States took the lead in the evolution of art. America became the melting pot of Cubism, Surrealism, Suprematism, Constructivism, and

59. Ludwig Mies van der Rohe.
Barcelona Chair. 1929.
Stainless steel frame,
seat covered in leather,
30×30×30".
Manufacturer: Knoll International

60. Jackson Pollock.
Number 1. 1948. 1948.
Oil on canvas, 68×104".
Collection, The Museum of Modern Art,
New York. Purchase

the European design movements. The ideas were assimilated into a culture with less clear-cut fiats, values, and depth of experience. The reality of the United States, though sobered by the Great Depression and World War II, did not demand that its artists mount a collective crusade. It could still entertain the luxury of individual expression founded on these European ideas and modified by a belief in the value of sociopsychological self-analysis.

These "artists-in-residence," among whom were Gropius, Mies van der Rohe, Albers, Mondrian, Duchamp, Gorky, De Kooning, Dali, and the prodigal Man Ray, all had a tremendous influence on the younger generation of American artists. Fertilized by this presence on their soil, American artists began a prodigious hybridization of the formal and conceptual seeds sown by the émigrés and their colleagues in Europe. Without a sentimental attachment to any one theory, American artists considered them all fair game and an erratic synthesis began. The barriers circumscribing the territory of "art" had been broken and individual artists took whatever formal, philosophical, or ethical tidbits served their personal obsessions.

After the Second World War, the work of artists like Pollock, Hofmann, Motherwell, and Still established the first truly American art form: Abstract Expressionism. Though still part of the modernist continuum, it flung down the gauntlet with the sheer physicality of its unrestrained emotional energy. It left the art lover stunned and appalled. It became the role of the gallery owner and the art critic to coax the public into understanding and acceptance of the new art. They soon assumed a formidable position of power and influence in determining the mainstream of art, even among artists. One of the most influential critics, Clement Greenberg, in his efforts to elucidate the proliferation of creative activity wrote in the late forties: "The essence of modernism lies, as I see it, in the use of the characteristic methods of a discipline to criticize the discipline itself—not in order to subvert it, but to entrench it more firmly in its area of competence.... Each art had to determine, through the operations peculiar to itself, the effects peculiar to itself."

Greenberg and his colleagues set the tone for the era and art seemed to narrow back in on itself, bent on formal innovation within the exclusive definitions of painting and sculpture. The ground-breaking merger of art and everyday life that had impassioned so many artists with its utopian possibilities in the first half of this century was abandoned. Art-making isolated itself in an ivory tower, measuring itself against its own immediate antecedents.

The fifties in America were characterized by rapid economic growth and the introduction of television into virtually every household. The printed media reflected the "good life" back to a largely patriotic society that took pride in its accomplishments. Without the need to rebuild, it could indulge in acquiring for itself all the earthly delights. Industry and technology had but to keep up with society's thirst for novelty.

American success had traditionally depended upon native efficiency and reliability, but an increasingly complex industrialization demanded greater standardization and conformity in the workplace. Jobs had to be clearly defined and compartmentalized within the bureaucracy and labor force. Though economic stability offered a greater share in the American dream, this "success" had its price.

The environment became the domain of architects and building contractors who, with some exceptions, bastardized the Bauhaus principles throughout the postwar building boom and transformed the contemporary environment into transient, prefabricated, rectilinear shells with bland and impersonal interiors.

In the art world, dealers and critics became the new arbiters of taste and proclaimed salient trends the way Detroit announced its latest model car. Each "ism" they enthroned seemed to automatically invite a modification or contradiction to supersede it. A hysteria of acquisition ensued among the affluent. Art openings became chic social events and art itself an investment commodity with the added appeal of public relations value.

Over the past thirty years, American artists have played out every self-referential variation on and departure from the immediately preceding trends in art. From Abstract Expressionism, where artists were totally "in" their painting, what followed over the next thirty years seemed determined to take the artist "out" of his work. There was the inevitable succession in sculpture and painting: Post-Painterly Abstraction, Assemblage, Color Field painting, Hard Edge Abstraction, Neo-Realism, Super-Realism, Op, Pop, Happenings, Performance Art, Body Art, Process Art, Pattern and Decoration, Site-Specific Art, Minimalism, Post-Minimalism, and, finally, Conceptual Art, which robbed the culture consumer of an art object altogether.

Some artists today have sensed a need once again for the painterly presence, and this could account for the still tentative popularity of the new work of the eighties, which reintroduces personal imagery and unabashedly draws from Expressionism, Futurism, and other proto-modernist styles. Even the recent trend of Post-modernist architecture has interjected a more humanist eclecticism into the arid urban environment.

It seems we have come full circle. The parallels between the social and cultural climates of the early part of our century and the present are striking. The industrial age, having run its course, is being replaced by an even more powerful and sophisticated technology. The nuclear age and the age of computer information are here, and although we are beginning to tame these new advances for our individual benefit, they are still threatening, mysterious, and remote for most of us.

Over the last thirty years national pride and self-confidence have been eroded by civil strife, assassination, violence and crime, wars, lowered standards of education, economic recession, unemployment, and the demise of established social programs. We are haunted by the specter of pollution and toxic waste, and global unrest brings the possibility of a Third World War ever closer.

In art, American modernism, with its self-proclaimed formalist criteria, has erected its own version of the academy. It has painted itself into a corner, and art is again regrettably out of sync with life. We find ourselves again in an era to be dealt with and yet that is the excitement of it. There has never been a more pressing mandate for artists to apply themselves to the task of revitalizing a dispirited society. But our society is infinitely more complex and unwieldy than it was sixty years ago and it is harder than ever to break through the inertia.

It was refreshing for me to circumvent the uncertainty of our culture and involve myself in an anomalous topic like artists' furniture. Over a three-year period, I recorded interviews with the artists of which you shall read excerpts. I questioned them about the motivations behind their making the pieces you shall see. Usually more reticent when discussing their art, the artists spoke in refreshingly candid and down-to-earth terms about their furniture. They got down to the fundamentals of the creative process and revealed their particular artistic sources and modi operandi. They spoke of the function of art in their daily lives and how they were applying its principles to improve them.

Furthermore, there was something solidly American in the testimony gleaned from these interviews. Taken as a whole, its general qualities included fierce individualism, ingenuity, innovation, enterprise, humor, and theatricality. There was an intrepid familiarity with modern technology that embraced or satirized it. There was a healthy independence from the constraints of traditional values. An Emersonian self-reliance, the most positive of deep-seated, time-honored American characteristics, seemed to be reaffirmed by these artists. What's more, my earlier hunch was correct: even though the functional requirements of the work presuppose built-in limitations, there was a wide variety of approaches, forms, and materials, all drawn largely from or indebted to the precedents I've outlined. In looking at the pieces it is possible to pick out the visual and philosophical transmogrifications of Cubism, Constructivism, De Stijl, the Bauhaus, and the individualistic, anthropomorphic, obsessive assemblages of Surrealism. There are constant echoes of Duchamp, but the humor and irony are American. The work also includes references to Oriental art and philosophy, Primitive Art, and early American furniture styles.

The more I pursued my research, the more I felt that this highly personal, narrowly defined cross-section of work—functional furniture—represented a humanizing, inspiring, and accessible body of purposeful creative activity. If it is the role of art to address itself to the spiritual deprivations of humanity in a specific time and to nourish our most profoundly human aspects, this unexpected work came to fulfill that need for me, whether or not it qualified for the pantheon of art.

Some of the furniture is intended for limited reproduction and takes into account the demands of manufacture; other pieces are unique. The craftsmanship may or may not be sophisticated. The materials may be precious or from the scrap heap. Most of the work stands in pointed opposition to the caveats of conventional furniture design. These artists have chosen, in their passionate use of materials, to convey an idea or an emotion. Personal taste aside, what is important are the issues that these pieces and their creators raise. The value of this furniture is, above all, conceptual.

The furniture suggests that the viable part of the modernist heritage in our complex time may not be so much the formalist lexicon of geometric abstraction as the liberating and idealistic philosophical premises of the Dadaist, Surrealist, and design movements of the twentieth century. They all recognized the active importance of art in the context of everyday living and returned the prerogative of aesthetic choice and expression to the individual. This furniture reminds us that we owe the best aspects of our environment today to those artists who singly and collectively pioneered the fusion of the principles of fine art to household objects. Those artists defended the position that the banal can be profound and that when it is we feel uplifted and human.

The functional furniture by artists gathered in this volume will hopefully delight and stimulate the reader, but its value lies in its potential to liberate us from our habitual responses, to broaden our expectations of functional forms, and to offer us a means of reclaiming our humanity. The artists represented in this book demonstrate that which is within everyone's reach today whatever the socio-economic position: to allow our senses to be uncritically captivated and our influences to simmer in our subconscious, to rebel against the banality that threatens a questioning, dynamic way of life, and boldly to manipulate our environments to suit our own individual needs.

D. D.

INTERVIEWS AND WORKS

61. Isamu Noguchi. *Coffee Table.* 1944.
Glass, wood, 15 × 50 × 36".
Manufactured by Herman Miller.
Courtesy the artist, Long Island City, New York

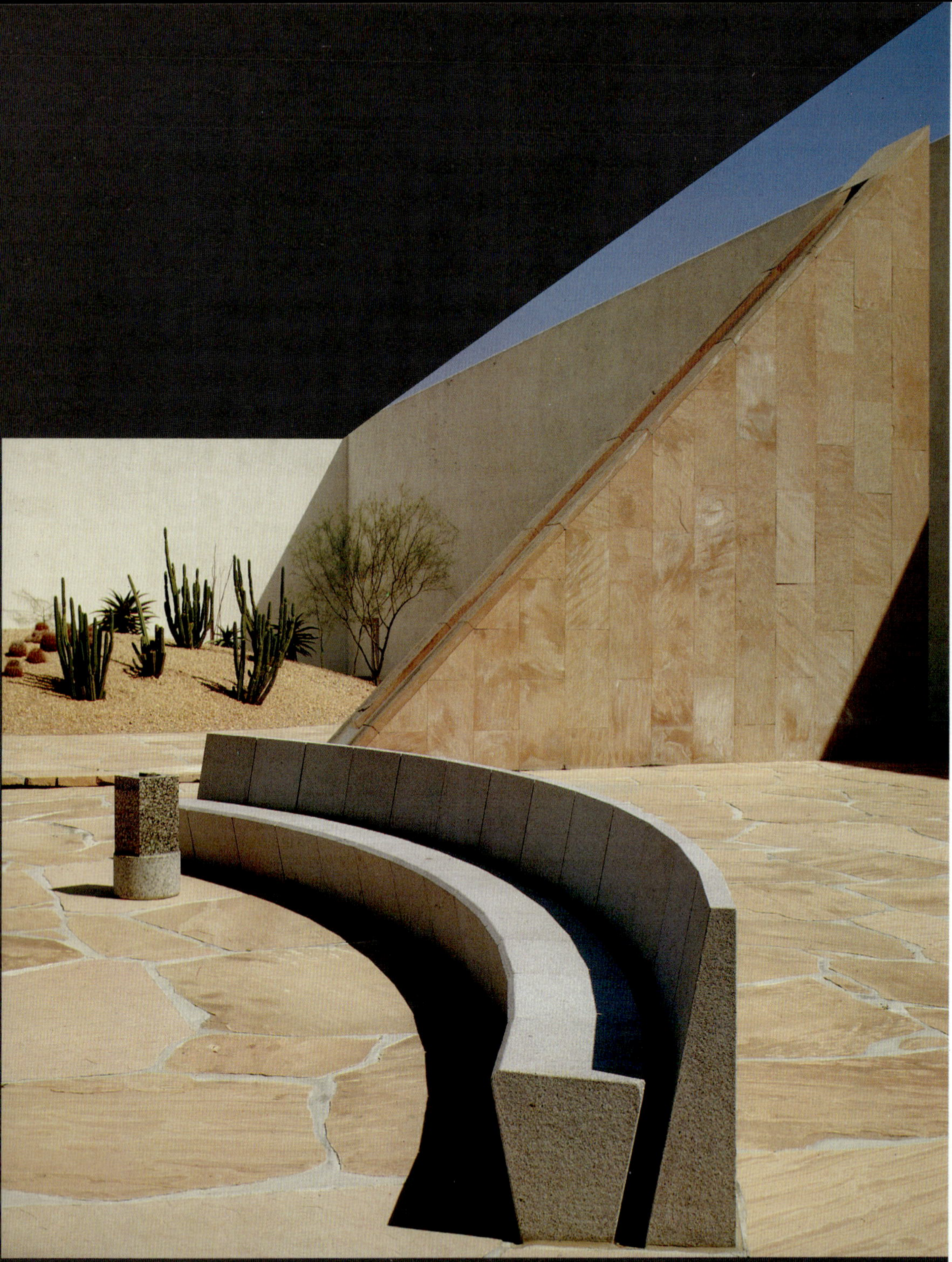

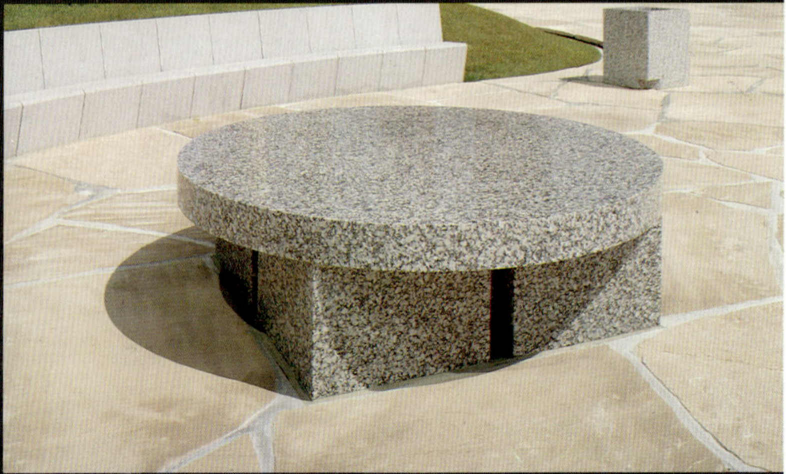

Isamu Noguchi

Born in Los Angeles, 1904
Lives in Long Island City,
New York, and Shikoku, Japan

Opposite, above:
62. Isamu Noguchi. *Bench*. 1980.
Granite, 26" × 27' × 34". Manufactured by the Cold Spring Granite Company for Two Town Center, Costa Mesa, California. Courtesy Fuller and Sadao PC, Architects, and the artist, Long Island City, New York

Opposite, below:
63. Isamu Noguchi. *Bench, Table, Trash Receptacle*. 1980. Granite, bench: 26" × 34' × 34"; table: 24 × 84"; trash receptacle: 32 × 26". Manufactured by the Cold Spring Granite Company for Two Town Center, Costa Mesa, California. Courtesy Fuller and Sadao PC, Architects, and the artist, Long Island City, New York

64. Isamu Noguchi.
Akari Lamps. 1951–52.
Mino (mulberry) paper, bamboo, wire, electrical fixtures, various sizes. Courtesy Sogetsu School of Flower Arrangement, Tokyo, Japan, and the artist, Long Island City, New York

It is clear that I often craved to bring sculpture into a more direct involvement with the common experience of living. At such times I felt there must be a more direct way of contact than the rather remote one of art. Initially this may have been no more than an attempt to move beyond the narrowing horizons of artistic sensibility. It bothered me that art so soon became a style with little creation added to its production. Why should the artistic imagination be so contained, or be unequal to the broadening scope of our world awareness? I thought of function as a determinator of form, and invention of function as a possible opening to an art beyond the accepted categories. Not art? Invention is equally creation to me.

Harry Anderson

Born in Highland Park, Illinois, 1943
Lives in Philadelphia

I was trained as an industrial designer and have always been interested in functional things and in people manipulating and interacting with the things I do. About 1970 I began collecting mass-produced objects —pottery, industrial tape dispensers, cameras, toys, light bulbs—and now this collecting has become the resource for my art. I present these items in installations that deal with the situation or environment in some way and convey a feeling that transcends the collection itself.

By contrast, the lamps I make are mostly combinations of my found objects and are single units that most likely will be sold and used. In that sense I consider them finished products of art.

The lamps here are more expressive than most that I make. I started to bend the shaft of one and it began to look like a stick figure, so I just carried the idea further. (I have always loved the image of H. C. Westermann's running figure.) I like the idea of my work being as useful as possible, but humorous rather than high tech. My work is serious, but it's funny, too.

65. Harry Anderson. *Three Lamps*. 1982.
Glass, neon, iron, plastic, brass.
Left to right: *Prometheus*, 48"; *Veronica*, 36"; *James*, 25".
Collection the artist, Philadelphia

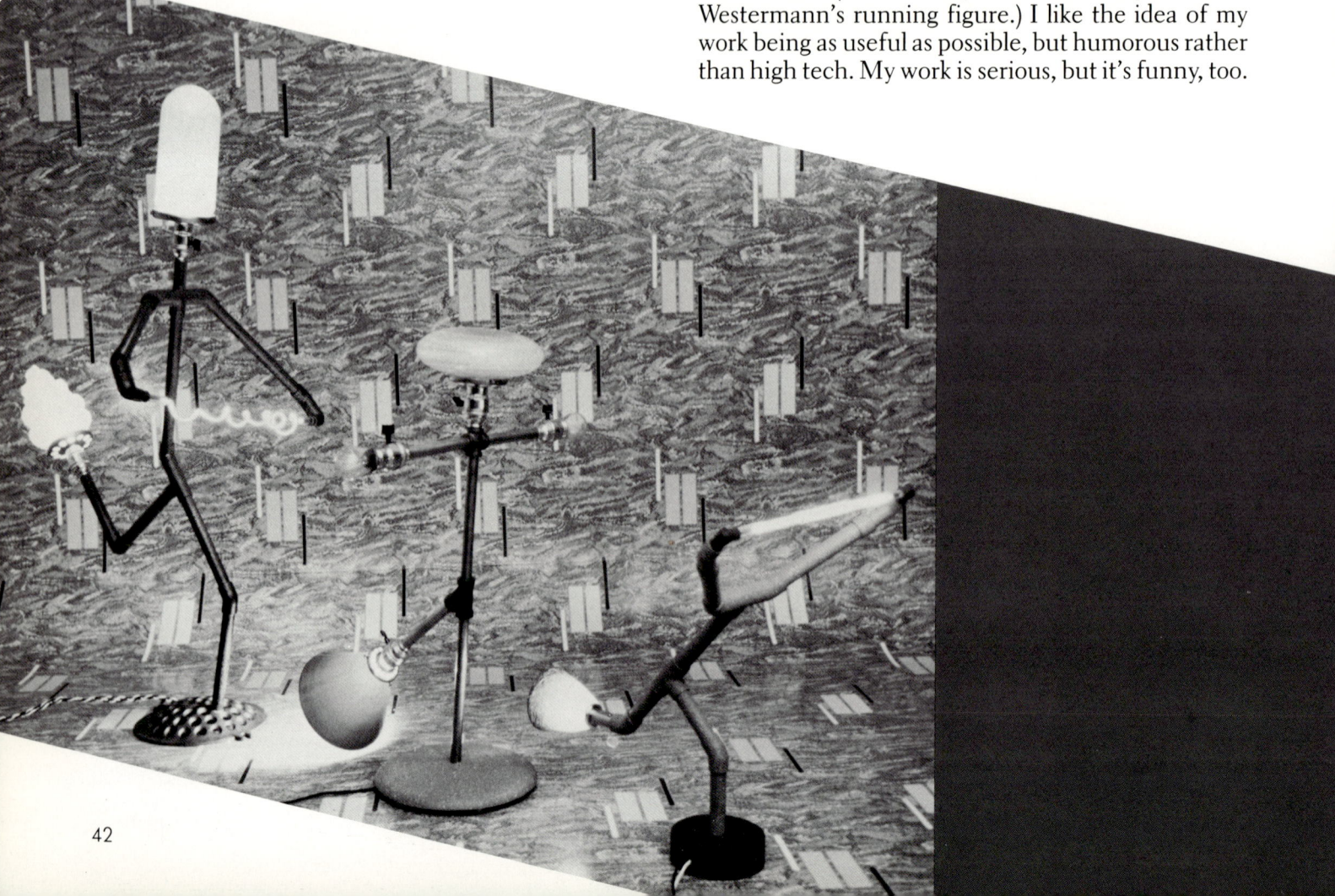

Lois Anderson

Born in Milwaukee, Wisconsin, 1927
Lives in Mill Valley, California

I'm a librarian by profession, but was inspired to make pieces like the ones shown here after I saw a car driving around Marin County covered entirely with statues and objects. "Gluing," a Bay Area phenomenon that started about fifteen years ago, is basically the ancient medium of mosaic work. It rang some sort of bell, and without any training I started doing it by myself. It was a perfect medium for me, and I've been using it now for almost thirteen years.

When I work on one of these pieces I have about sixty boxes of things I've collected around me. I've always been a collector. My eye never stops at a flea market or rummage sale. I look for stuff you wouldn't believe: junky frames, buttons, costume jewelry, statues.... It takes about a week to know where everything is, and then it takes anywhere from one to six months to make one.

Because I am strongly influenced by Oriental and religious art, a kaleidoscope of religious figures and dancers adorn my pieces. Making the pieces is a form of meditation for me, a kind of spiritual search I do with my hands. I like reverence, and it makes me feel good to make something colorful, balanced, awe-inspiring, monumental, and flamboyant—and then have it around me. People tell me I'm a temple artist in the wrong place, and jokingly I tell them I'm in the Tantric furniture business.

44

Opposite:
66. Lois Anderson.
The Dresser. 1974.
Found dresser, beads, rhinestones, jewelry, shells, statues, plaques, 78 × 60 × 24".
Collection the Oakland Museum, California

67. Lois Anderson.
The Buddha Lamp. 1972.
Wooden pedestal, Buddha lamp, records, rhinestones, jewelry, statues, icons, beads, 84 × 24 × 18".
Collection the artist,
Mill Valley, California

68. Richard Artschwager. *Chair and Table*. 1980. Formica on wood, metal handle, chair: 41 × 21½ × 24"; table: 32 × 48 × 36". Courtesy Leo Castelli Gallery, New York

Richard Artschwager

Born in Washington, D.C., 1924
Lives in New York

69. Richard Artschwager. *Bookcase III*. 1981.
Wood, 26½ × 36 × 6".
Courtesy Leo Castelli Gallery, New York

I studied biology, switched to art, spent time in the service, and then had to find a way to make a living. One day I passed a lumber yard, walked in, saw great planks of mahogany, and knew what I had to do. Making furniture in a workshop environment would provide a balanced diet of action and reflection, and it was a real job. What I made was, in the most ordinary sense, needed by others, so I had a morally tenable connection to society.

Ten years later and a little more than twenty years ago, I commenced to make some furniture as art. The jangles and resonances created by the slightest deviation from the regular factory production were illuminating. I wanted to make an image in space that didn't need a privileged place like a painting. It was the kind of credibility I could live with while still being a cabinetmaker.

At the outset I made the furniture solely for myself, not for an audience or for accreditation in the corporate sensibility of art. It was intended to bridge the gap between functional and nonfunctional. That was my interest and that was my radicalism. Its forms were not dictated but were offered up by virtue of where I was in the furniture workshop and by what materials I had available. Very consciously I allowed those things to determine what got done. I was enchanted with the idea of how art arises as opposed to the notion of art as a received body of art history, criticism, and accredited works.

The formalism of my art is about eliciting a response of speculation and fantasy in the viewer through certain kinds of sensory deprivations.

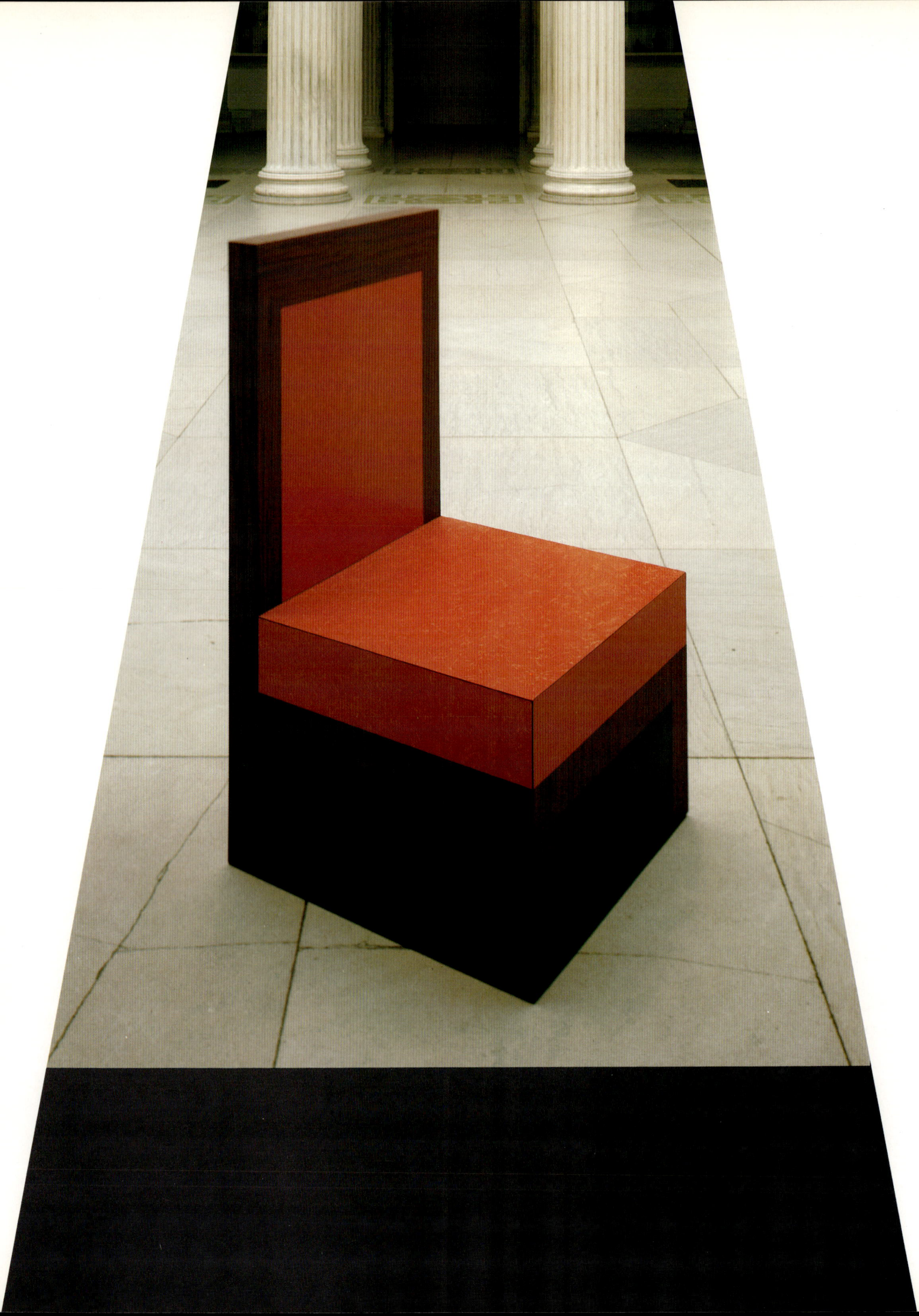

Opposite:
70. Richard Artschwager. *Chair.* 1963.
Formica on wood, 37 × 20 × 22".
Courtesy Leo Castelli Gallery, New York

71. Richard Artschwager. *Table with Pink Tablecloth.* 1964.
Formica on wood, 25¼ × 44 × 44".
Courtesy Leo Castelli Gallery, New York

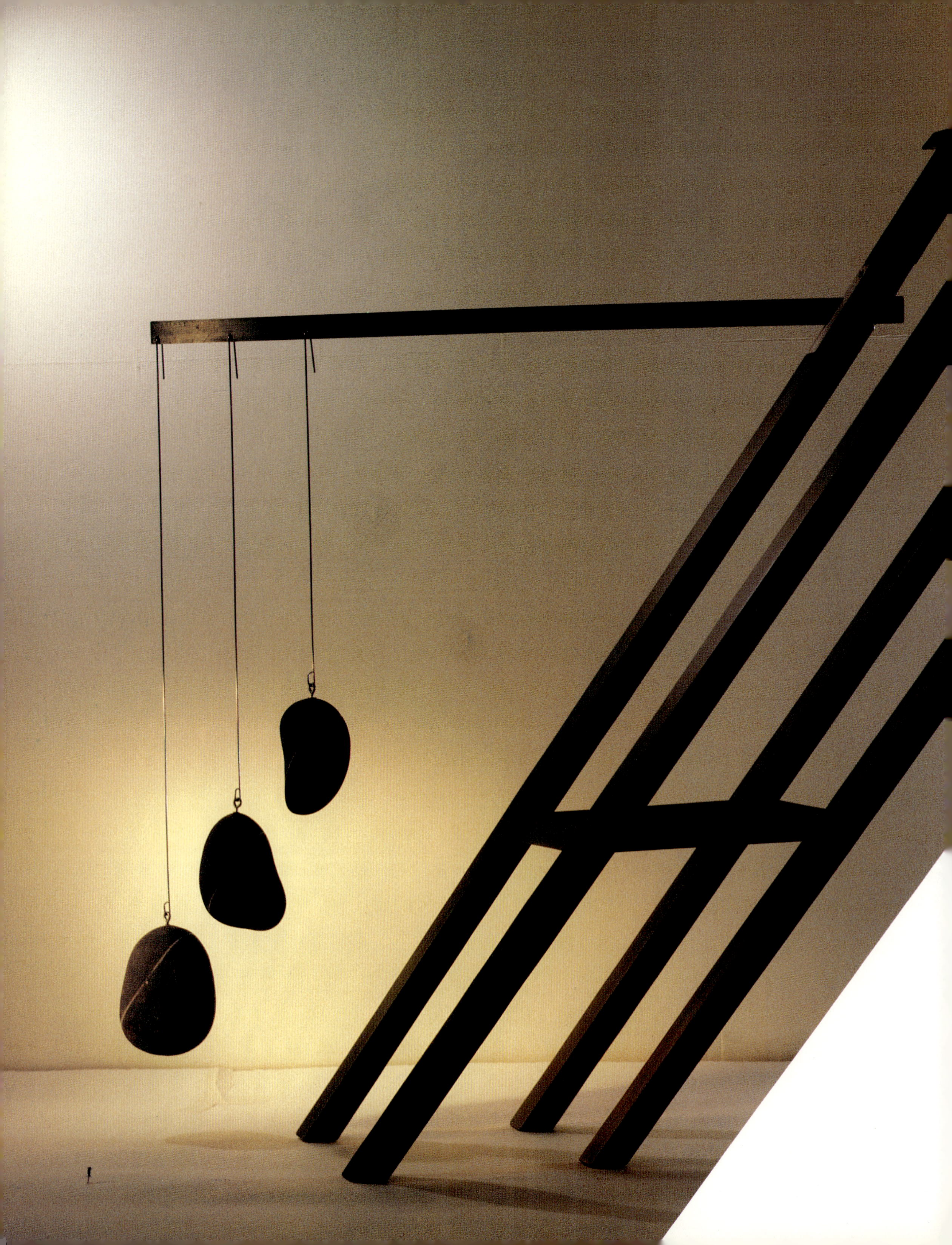

Rafael Barrios

Born in Baton Rouge, Louisiana, 1947
Lives in New York and Caracas, Venezuela

72. Rafael Barrios.
Mesa Table. 1978.
Wood, paint, 19 × 30 × 11".
Art et Industrie, New York

73. Rafael Barrios.
Rock Table. 1977.
River rocks,
stainless steel,
wood, paint, 52 × 72 × 18".
Collection Museum of Contemporary Art, Caracas, Venezuela

I've always loved furniture. I had a business for a while with my sister in Venezuela designing offices that folded up—desk, typewriter, and all—into eight-by-ten modules that could be put on a truck and easily moved. That got me into furniture, and I started spending a lot of time on ergonomics and notions of the extension of man.

My tables were inspired by my previous sculpture. I've always been involved in balance, gravity, vertigo, deformation. My work has always had at least a functional connotation, and that has to do with a social concern I have about art being accessible. The whole idea of deformation has to do with how much what exists and has existed historically influences our way of life, starting with the ubiquitous ninety-degree angle. There has always been that linear, perpendicular thinking. The work I make is about delivering us from the kinds of historical conditioning that obstruct creativity and art. Whether I'm doing sculpture, painting, or design, my primary concern is to transform, renew. Sticking to optics and axiometrics has to do with transforming the perspective in which you see the space that you live in and how that affects you physiologically.

Below:
74. Larry Bell.
Table de Lux I. 1981.
Carpathian elm burl,
30 × 55½ × 55½". Collection the artist,
Taos, New Mexico

Larry Bell

Born in Chicago, 1939
Lives in Taos, New Mexico

75. Larry Bell.
Chair de Lux IV. 1981.
Carpathian elm burl, bird's-eye maple,
cotton velvet, 32 × 26 × 32".
Collection the artist, Taos, New Mexico

The motivation for making furniture came from a long-postponed desire to reproduce an old chair I had purchased for twenty dollars in a junk store years ago. What I hadn't realized was that so many other kinds of pieces based on the shape of that chair had been brewing in my mind. So as the designer I enlisted an excellent woodworker and an excellent upholsterer.

First we pulled the chair apart to see the shaping of the understructure. The design of the chair was based on a quartered forty-degree ellipse. There were subtleties inside that were not apparent on the outside. The materials of the original chair were so beautiful that there was no point in changing them for the new pieces. We found the same veneer and even located the same cotton velvet made by a company in France that has been making it for the last hundred years.

I'm not in the furniture business. The furniture is part of my everyday work process. I'm not going to say that it's sculpture, but I certainly can't separate the desire to do it and the kinds of decisions that go into the making of my furniture from the desire and decisions that go into the making of my sculpture. I take the position that art is a teacher, that the physical things that manifest themselves through this learning process are the vehicle for learning. I don't separate any of the stuff I do from my art, and in this way everything in my life is integrated into my studio activities.

76. Larry Bell. *Furniture de Lux Living Room.* 1980–81.
Carpathian elm burl, bird's-eye maple, cotton velvet,
glass, aluminum, silicon monoxide.

77. Billy Al Bengston. *Solvang Screen*. 1982. Five panels, inlay wood, 78 × 90".
Fabricator: Greg Erickson. Collection Michael McCarty/Michael's Restaurant, Santa Monica, California

Billy Al Bengston

Born in Dodge City, Kansas, 1934
Lives in Los Angeles

I'm not domestic, I'm not a dog. I don't roll up at your feet, but I like where I live, and I take a hand in it all the time. I'm constantly adjusting, and I couldn't survive without doing that.

I became involved in working on both sides of my paintings, and then the idea for screens just materialized. I don't know why a painting has to hang on the wall, and I don't know why you should have to look at it all the time. It should be something you can fold up and put away or hide something behind when company comes. That's why I thought the screens were a good idea, and I still do.

I'm also a table man. I used to make a table just about every day. Tables are part of the work ethic, part of the everyday thing. I like working with wood, and I'm good with it, but I don't have time to do everything anymore. I have too many ideas, so who needs to do it when you can get somebody else to do it? It's the American way, and we have to do it the American way.

Furniture is furniture; I never considered it art. I figure if anybody else can do it, it isn't art. That's where I draw the line. To paraphrase Ad Reinhardt, furniture is what you back into when you're looking at a painting.

78. Billy Al Bengston.
Left: *Iki Lawai'a*. 1982.
Wood, 19×33×9½".
Right: *Iki Pua'a*. 1982.
Wood, 17×17×17".
Fabricator: Greg Erickson.
Courtesy Billy Al Bengston Studio, Venice, California

79. Scott Burton. *Acrylic Chair*. 1981–82.
Acrylic, 41 × 23½ × 29".
Courtesy Max Protetch Gallery, New York

80. Scott Burton. *Rock Chair*. 1980–82.
Granite, 39 × 32 × 42".
Private collection, Philadelphia

Opposite, left:
82. Scott Burton.
Storage Cubes I. 1979–80.
Wood, lacquer, hinges,
40½ × 30 × 30".
Collection Barry Lowen,
Los Angeles

Opposite, far right:
83. Scott Burton.
Seat and Table. 1982.
Polished granite,
seat: 20 × 24 × 15";
table: 28 × 17 × 12½".
Collection Robert H. Halff,
Los Angeles

81. Scott Burton. *Steel Furniture*. 1979.
Rusted, lacquered steel,
chair: 32×17×17";
table: 29×55×26";
stool/table: 18×19¾×10¾";
bench/table: 18×38×17".
Courtesy Daniel Weinberg Gallery,
San Francisco/Los Angeles

Scott Burton

Born in Greensboro, Alabama, 1939
Lives in New York

84. Scott Burton. *Onyx Table*. 1978–81.
Onyx, steel armature, fluorescent lights, 29×60×60".
Collection Charles and Doris Saatchi, London

When I first decided to become an artist as an adolescent, I did mostly paintings and drawings, but I was equally interested in architecture and design. Now I am also fascinated by the theater and dance, and it's that range, from design to theater, that interests me as an artist.

Tableau is a form I identify with. Beginning in 1970 I did furniture installations: tableaux in forests, on stages, in galleries. I still stage performances: tableaux with real people. In 1973, however, I decided that I really wanted to design furniture instead of continuing to use found, "readymade" pieces. Also I wanted to design furniture for everyday use in the home rather than pieces removed from use in the context of tableaux or museum exhibitions. It was not an easy decision to make and was misunderstood at first. The subject matter of my work now is in the common terms of furniture and there is that implication of a broader accessibility.

For the most part furniture today is in sad shape. As an artist rather than a real designer or craftsperson, I have the freedom and the opportunity to invent a whole new style of furniture for my place and time in American history. Contemporary designs are mostly pastiches of the modernist classics, and organic crafts furniture is no more authentic or fresh, and promotes illusory, sentimental values. I want to be neither a corporate hireling nor an aging hippie. I believe that furniture should not be negative or critical or falsely complacent. I want my work to express optimistic values.

Designers of furniture need to have some common sense, whereas I rarely abandon an idea on the grounds of impracticality. I don't have to think in rational terms; I can do whatever I like. The result is that certain work finds its place only in the art world. But I feel very lucky that, at this point in history, what I love best has a new, wider significance. A friend of mine, Edit deAk, once wrote about me and ended with a paraphrase of Gertrude Stein: "Scott. Chairs. Eloquently." That is how I would like my epitaph to read.

85. Wendell Castle. *Table with Cloth*. 1980.
Mahogany, 34 × 30½ × 18".
Courtesy Alexander F. Milliken, Inc., New York

86. Wendell Castle.
Octagonal Table. 1983.
Bird's-eye maple and ebony,
height 22"; diameter 33".
Courtesy Alexander F. Milliken, Inc.,
New York

Wendell Castle

Born in Emporia, Kansas, 1932
Lives in Scottsville, New York

87. Wendell Castle.
Collector's Cabinet. 1981.
French pearwood, ebony,
63 × 17 × 17".
Collection the artist,
Scottsville, New York

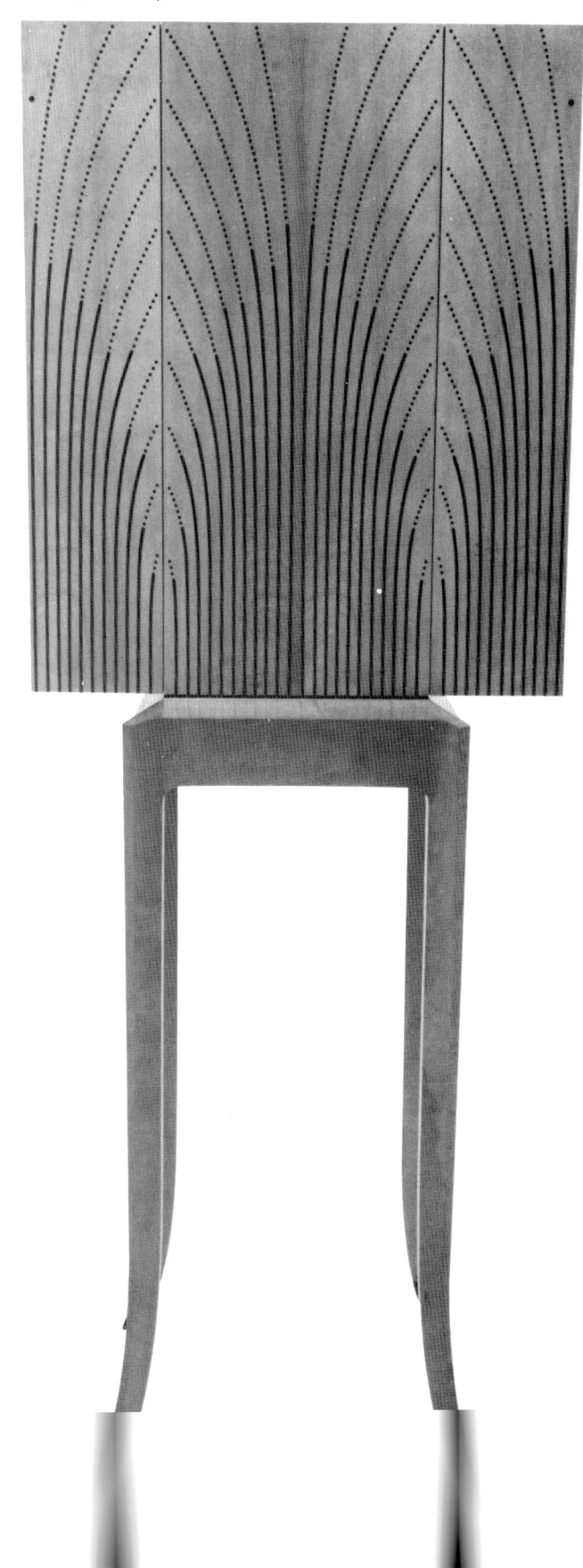

Until about five years ago my furniture was almost exclusively organic forms. I came from a sculptural background and started making furniture in the late fifties, experimenting with lamination techniques. When I moved to New York and began teaching, I had access to tools and equipment that allowed me to develop more precise and sophisticated techniques. Lamination was not new, but I was the first to develop its use in furniture. I taught the technique to a lot of people and the style spread. About 1969 I started to feel that my work was too pervasive. Lamination was getting a bad name because people did not understand it, and it had deteriorated. About six years ago I decided to write a book on the subject and quit teaching lamination.

I became involved with trompe-l'oeil woodcarvings, and those pieces were automatically accepted as a different art form even though they looked more like furniture than the earlier work. I never considered any of my furniture to be sculpture, but people said that these pieces were art. It was sort of a turnaround. I always considered my work a sculpturelike activity, but it has always been furniture.

Very recently I became involved with furniture that is very clearly in the furniture tradition, and does not appear in the remotest sense to look like sculpture. The new furniture has its basis in historical styles. It's a sort of random and unlikely rearrangement of elements and references to Jacobean, Empire, Louis XV, Louis XVI, Roman, Greek, and so forth. It is elaborately made of exotic woods and fancy materials. I work with a team of five who combine special skills. I design, coordinate, work on the pieces, and make the final decisions.

I feel that a piece must have presence and attract your attention at some critical distance away from it. Secondly it must have a diversity of scale so that as you walk closer and become more involved with it, what you see from a distance will go out of focus and new sets of things will come into focus.

I think there has been almost no fine furniture made since the twenties. I consider Emile Ruhlmann to be one of the last great cabinetmakers. The Bauhaus was concerned with a machine aesthetic and production, and I'm against the machine-made

John Chamberlain

Born in Rochester, Indiana, 1927
Lives in Sarasota, Florida

I started making couches about 1969 or 1970. I needed some place to sit down, which is the best reason for making them, I suppose. I had this material that had been something else, so I sort of carved it out with a couple of slim knives.

The idea of the couch is essentially to alter your sitting consciousness, to sit around like you did when you were eight. Other than that the scale allows a number of people to get on one all at once. I did one that was forty feet by twelve feet by four feet high.

In making these couches there were a lot of problems to solve. It was necessary to have a certain amount of mass. I had to learn to get that mass through thirty-inch doors, order the foam, tie it together, glue it, and cover it to keep it from disintegrating. Those were the logistics in terms of the material itself and the maintenance and upkeep. The couches must be covered, the more the better, with anything you want to throw on them.

I used to do three or four a year by commission for somebody in a particular place. They're great fun to make. I'm still making them. Kids and dogs like them a lot.

88. John Chamberlain. *Thordis's Barge*. 1980-81.
Urethane foam, fabric, 29½ × 11'6" × 12'8".
© Dia Art Foundation 1982, New York

Colette
(a.k.a. Justine)

Born in Tunis, Tunisia, 1947
Lives in New York

I have used my living environment as an inner sculpture, continuously transforming it, reconstructing it, recovering it, making my body in relationship to my home analogous to an animal living in its shell. What began as a conceptual work of art became for me an endless source of inspiration for music, fashion, interior design, and architecture.

For the past twelve years I have created many womblike environments similar to the one I live in and have installed them in museums, galleries, streets, shop windows, and nightclubs. I have often appeared in them as an integral part of the work. Certain elements have recurred in these rooms, although the themes have varied according to the space and energy of the site. Each was totally constructed with draped, crinkled, or crushed silks and similar fabrics. They were monochromatic, had mirrors placed especially to create illusion, light sources and photographs embedded in the fabric, and audios usually composed of voices. These rooms were short-lived, and their relics were recycled into art objects.

I have been exploring ways in which function and strong visual impact can coexist. Though my approach is different, my ambitions are similar to Bauhaus ideals. But in contrast to the coldness of contemporary design, I want to create an atmosphere of simplicity and warmth, very modern, yet ancient. I use fabric to create a feeling of softness, humanity, and emotional energy. The furniture is entirely covered in the same fabric and installed electronically so it disappears, avoiding clutter. In a way, one could describe it as "Minimal baroque."

89. Colette (a.k.a. Justine). *My House*. 1980.
Rusched silks, satins,
lights, photographs, 15 × 50′.
Courtesy the artist, New York

Arch Connelly

Born in Chicago, 1950
Lives in New York

90. Arch Connelly. *Dark Pool*. 1982.
Rhinestones, pearls, glass,
acrylic paint, wood, papier-mâché,
22 × 28 × 24".
Courtesy the artist,
New York

I consider myself a sculptor. Even when I paint I think of my work in terms of objects. I wanted to make sculpture that had a utilitarian function as well as a purely aesthetic one because I always felt it was silly to make sculpture that didn't do anything.

Furniture should function on as many levels as possible. Whether these pieces are seen as sculpture or merely as tables is fine, but it makes it better if people can integrate the two and get involved in the ambiguity of form, function, and aesthetic possibilities.

I've been through the sixties, seventies, high tech, and so on. I like geometry, but I reject the coldness of Minimalism. The whimsy of rococo, Futurism, and artists like Calder and Westermann have influenced me a great deal. I love the heavy emotion and overdone darkness of nineteenth-century art. I consider myself a Mannerist since I use so many ideas borrowed from the past. Though I love theatricality and utilize kitsch, my criteria is not based on making fun of things. I believe in the decorative and that things must be beautiful. I'm a stickler for craftsmanship and to me what I do is well crafted.

I amass elements and they stay around the studio for months until I understand how best to utilize them and what kinds of associations I want. The idea of things being underwater appeals to me; an aquarium is a picture or little diorama, and like museum-type imagery it has a certain very defined kind of space that you look into, so I use aquarium supplies. They are mass produced and all the same predefined shapes that I can use repeatedly in different permutations as basic forms. I like the fact that people can bring their associations to them, although my recent work uses more abstract materials so the reaction can be on a more aesthetic level.

91. Arch Connelly. *Cubist Table*. 1980.
Lumilar, aquarium gravel, auto paint,
aluminum leaf, plastic on wood, 36 × 27 × 20".
Collection Jedd Garet, New York

Ron Cooper/Robert Mangurian

Born in New York, 1943
Lives in Taos, New Mexico

Born in Baltimore, Maryland, 1941
Lives in Venice, California

The idea for making furniture evolved from the materials themselves because there is a curious kind of plane that is defined by a sheet of glass. I asked Robert if we could work together on the furniture because I respected what he had done in architecture. We collaborated for the joy of stepping out of our own disciplines and being able to play aesthetically in neutral territory.

The furniture is basically a manipulation of a vertical plane and two horizontal planes with the added variable of grid, diagonal, or parallel lines. I had already been using the grid in my art, relating it to the history of painting and photography. Robert and I found that we could create illusions similar to looking into the corner of a cube. This process had the quality of playing with illusion and gravity and antigravity. Robert also liked the tradition in architecture of making fake materials, like imitating marble, so the zolotone rectangle painted underneath the glass parodies the green leather, or blotters, of old desk tops. The pinstripes on the surface are like lines for penmanship. One could conceivably put a plain white piece of paper on top of it, and it would have perfectly ruled lines. The supports at the back have the traditional compartments of an old roll-top desk. These pay homage to historical works and bring up the issue of organization as well as add an interesting design relief.

92. Ron Cooper and Robert Mangurian. *Wire Glass Desk*. 1980.
Wire glass, silicon rubber, zolotone paint, 30 × 60 × 36".
Collection G. Tilton Gardner, Santa Monica, California

Guy de Cointet

Born in Paris, France, 1934
Lives in Los Angeles, New York, and Paris

In my performance pieces there is a progression in the dialogue, but there is nothing so striking as plot. I'm not interested in the theater for the theater. I'm interested in setting up an ambience or an environment and in having people talk. What I like is the texture of the characters interacting with the objects and shapes and feeling completely at ease with them. There is as much variation in the way the characters talk as there is in all the objects, and they go together in close relationship to each other. The audience sees arrangements and piles of painted geometric forms. During the course of my plays these forms are talked about and their identities revealed. After the audience discovers what everything is, sometimes they're even more confused.

My furniture designs for the sets of my performances evolve with respect to their effect on stage because that is their first function. If they function well as a set, they should be okay to live with, with very little alteration. In fact I use them as much as I can in my studio between performances.

In the play *A New Life*, the *Preparation Armchair* doesn't really look like a seat. It is really very comfortable because you don't need a back when you can lean on two sides. In *De Toutes les Couleurs*, a play I did in Paris, the shapes are quite playful. The books are exactly the same size and shape as the backs of the chairs. Before this I always made tables with four legs, but I found that eliminating them created less shadow and didn't interfere with the legs of the actors.

94. Guy de Cointet.
Preparation Armchair. 1981.
Painted wood, 30 × 25 × 10½".
Collection Rene Ricard,
New York

93. Guy de Cointet.
Set for *De Toute les Couleurs*, Theatre du Rond-Point, Paris. 1982.
Furniture, walls, door, and window: painted wood; other props: painted cardboard.
Courtesy Yves Lefevbre Productions, Paris

Stephen de Staebler

Born in St. Louis, Missouri, 1933
Lives in Berkeley, California

95. Stephen de Staebler.
Dark Throne. 1977.
High-fired clay, 34 × 29 × 23".
Collection the artist,
Berkeley, California

Making chairs came directly out of my attempts to make nonfunctional sculpture in the early sixties. Back then I wanted to make figures out of clay that would stand up. Because clay is so affected by gravity, I had to use the intermediate level of a figure sitting down. I wanted to keep the clay fresh so I could build the figure lying down and lift it into a sitting position piece by piece. I wasn't setting out to make a chair, but inadvertently I was making chair forms to take the seated figure. That was the beginning of the idea for a seat. In 1967 I was commissioned to do the sanctuary of the Newman Center in Berkeley. I realized that I had been looking for some way to fuse sculpture with the environment. The work fell into place unlike the struggles of the figure/chair form.

The commission for the University of California Art Museum at Berkeley was an extension of the idea of segmented landscape forms that were shaped more to accommodate the body. To make that grouping I made three big mountain forms in my studio, ten or twelve feet across. After the mountain forms had been established I cut them up into sections while the clay was still soft enough to shape. Some looked like thrones, some like hunks of rock, but one way or another they all functioned as something to sit on.

I've found that most furniture gets established in some kind of grid pattern, so for the commission I intentionally placed these elements askew, playing with oblique spatial relationships that would force total strangers to tolerate closeness and to interact.

In making these pieces—which I often make for myself as well—I want the clay to live and not be killed off by overmanipulation. I use stains and oxides and the color of the clays rather than glazes. The whole tonality is very important and has a wonderful richness to it. I've always felt that making the thrones was completing a cycle in my work because it stands somewhere between my attraction toward landscape, nonobjective form, and my involvement with the human figure.

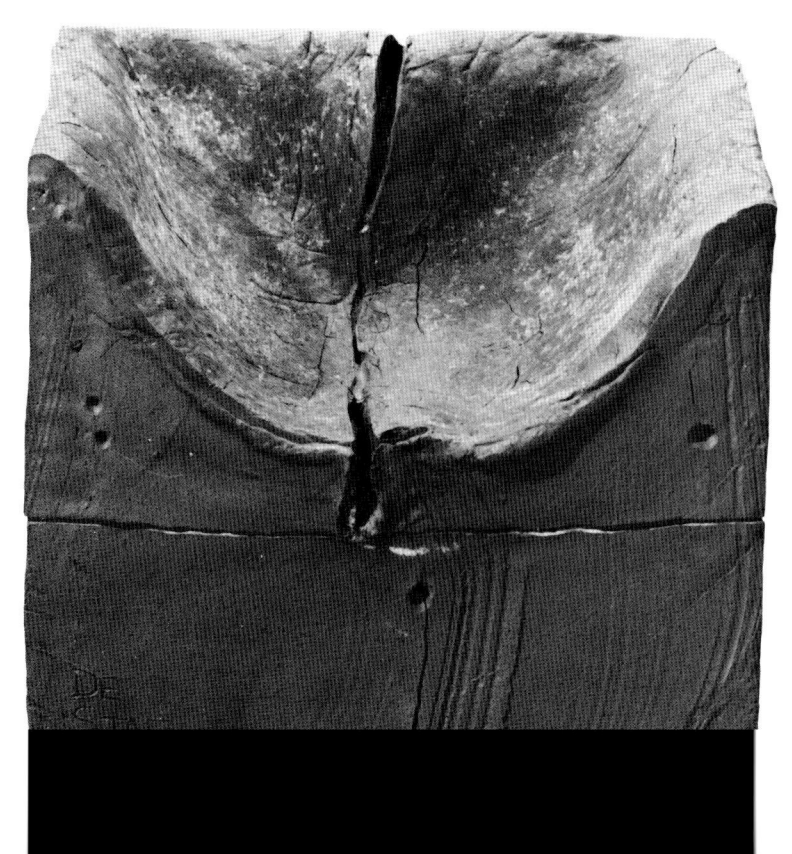

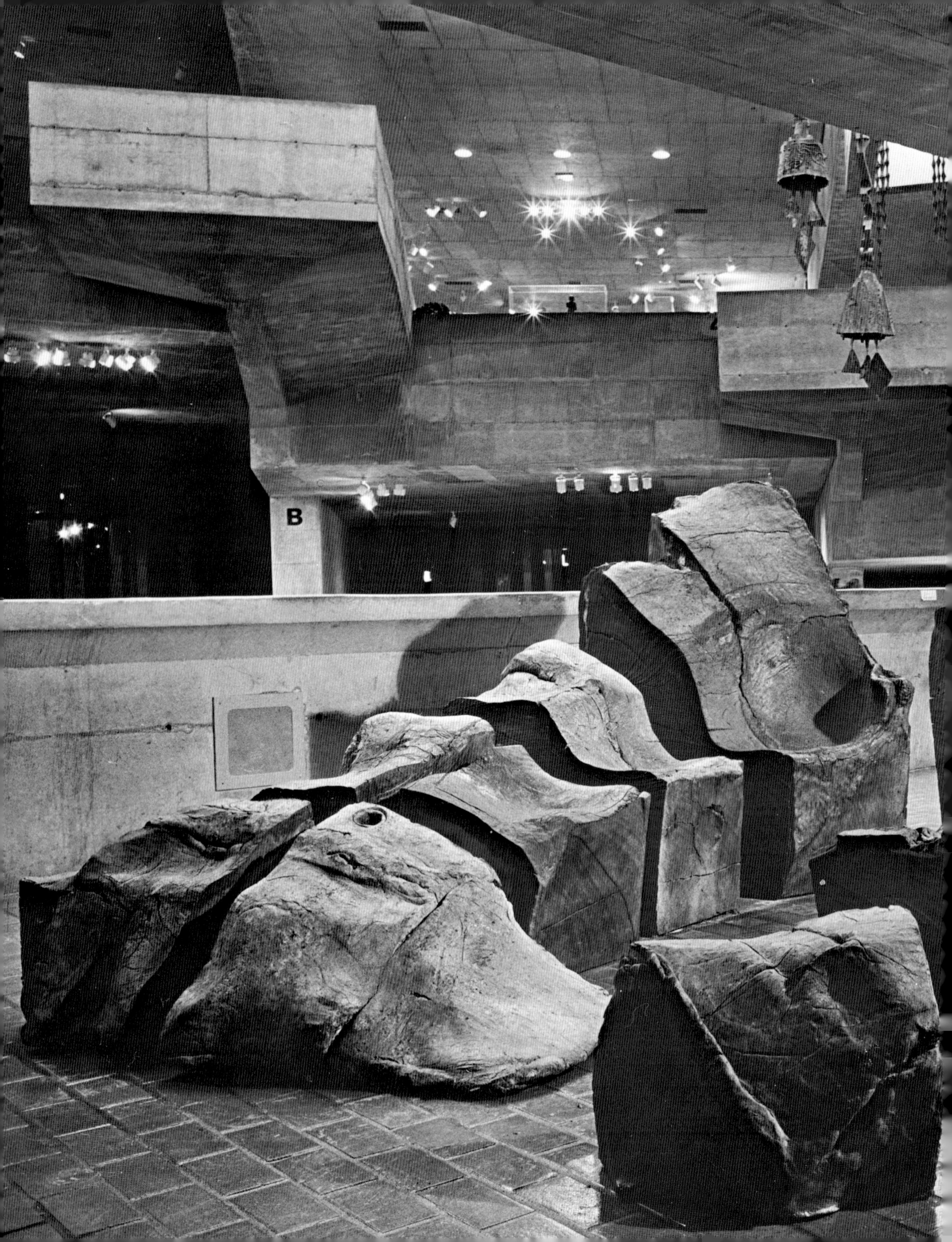
B

96. Stephen de Staebler. *Seating Environment.* 1970.
High-fired clay (thirty-two sections).
Courtesy University Art Museum, University of California, Berkeley

97. Stephen de Staebler.
Valentine Throne. 1974.
Stoneware, low-fired clay,
42 × 33 × 30".
Courtesy Oakland Museum,
California

Jim Dine

Born in Cincinnati, Ohio, 1935
Lives in Putney, Vermont

I have a great interest in furniture, and through the years I've collected lots of different kinds. I like Georgian and Chippendale, and furniture of exceptional quality, as well as simple Adirondack and Mexican furniture, which is strange and eccentric and has been made out of nothing in particular. I find that these pieces move me tremendously. The charge is as good as what I get from sculpture or fine art. When I go to museums I don't just look at paintings; I look at furniture and how things are joined. It is very inspiring and a primary source material for my work. For me furniture is like sculpture, metaphors for people, the same way tools are.

I have the ability to be a primitive carpenter, but joinery doesn't interest me as an activity. I've done a lot of furniture for my own use, but it hasn't been showable. The boot bench was one of the pieces that I daydreamed. The boots were from another piece of sculpture, and I just put them at either end of a board and cast the whole thing in sand. The mirror has objects—an axe, a wrench, tin snips—that were part of the reliefs I was making at the time. I work in series, and one thing feeds another. When I make sculpture it is easy to use the components and put them together in another way.

I come from earlier art, from a long line of artists, and this is what I care about. I pit myself against the past; the future is not the competition in my life, and I don't see anything that inspires me there. I realize this isolates me in a way, but I'm concerned with building upon my sources, my roots as an artist.

98. Jim Dine. *Mirror.* 1976.
Cast polyester resins, gold leaf, mirror, 31 × 50".
Courtesy Biltmore Hotel, Los Angeles

99. Jim Dine. *A Boot Bench Ochre #2.* 1965.
Cast aluminum, 71 × 17½ × 12".
Collection Mr. and Mrs. Alfred R. Stern

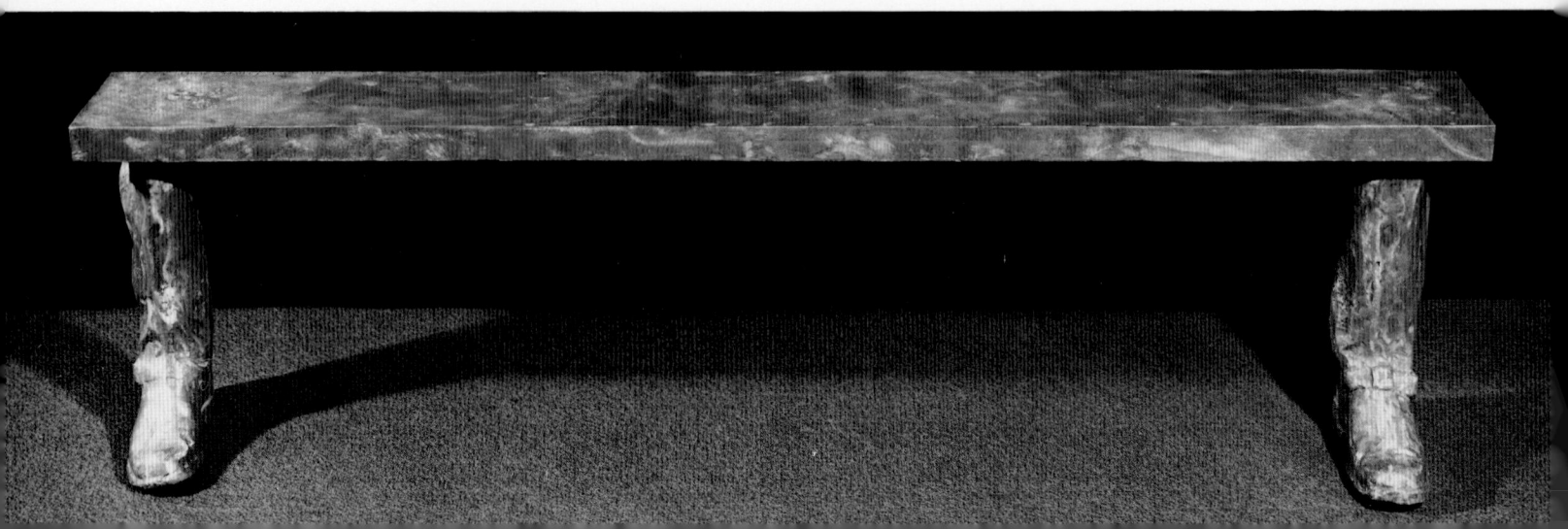

100. Mark di Suvero.
Mirrored Rolling Cabinet with Painting on Back. 1976.
Plywood, mirror, paint, castors, 71 × 98¾ × 28".
Swinging Bed. 1975. Wood, cable, 27½ × 83 × 64".
Chair. 1980. Wood, 20½ × 46 × 8¾".
Courtesy Oil & Steel Gallery,
New York, and
the artist

Mark di Suvero

Born in Shanghai, China, 1933
Lives in Petaluma, California,
and New York

Some people call these pieces furniture, but I call them "rides," "interactional sculpture." When I say "interactional" I mean the opposite of that kind of cold, trite, pristine art that you can't touch or get involved with. Eliminating that barrier is a very important part of my art. I wanted my work to be physically felt, and I started with the "rides" as something completely separate. Now I sometimes incorporate them into my sculpture.

It seems to me that most of the furniture around is very unimaginative. If you look at it from a Martian point of view, people are caught in a physiological vise. Furniture is a kind of symbolic imposition of control. It controls not only the way a person lives but the behavior of those who enter into the space. When you walk into a Louis XIV room, you behave. What I try to do is give people maximum mobility and a certain sense of freedom. My furniture is subversive of that rigorous control. For instance, after you have slept on a swinging bed, going back to a stationary one is a definite step down. I tend to make a swinging bed wherever I live because it does something: it works on your sense of balance, like a cradle, and most people are transported. Being picked up and moved in this oscillating motion is very rare once you're grown up. It brings you back to preracial consciousness, evolutionarily, when we were swinging from trees. It's also incredible for lovemaking.

As for the rolling cabinet, I designed it but did not build it. I think that when one designs something and doesn't do it, the piece comes out differently. But the cabinet was a very interesting painting to do. It was inspired by mystical thoughts. The big mirrors on the doors really change the room; mirrors are usually fixed in a house, but when you can turn them and move them around, you suddenly see the space in many different ways.

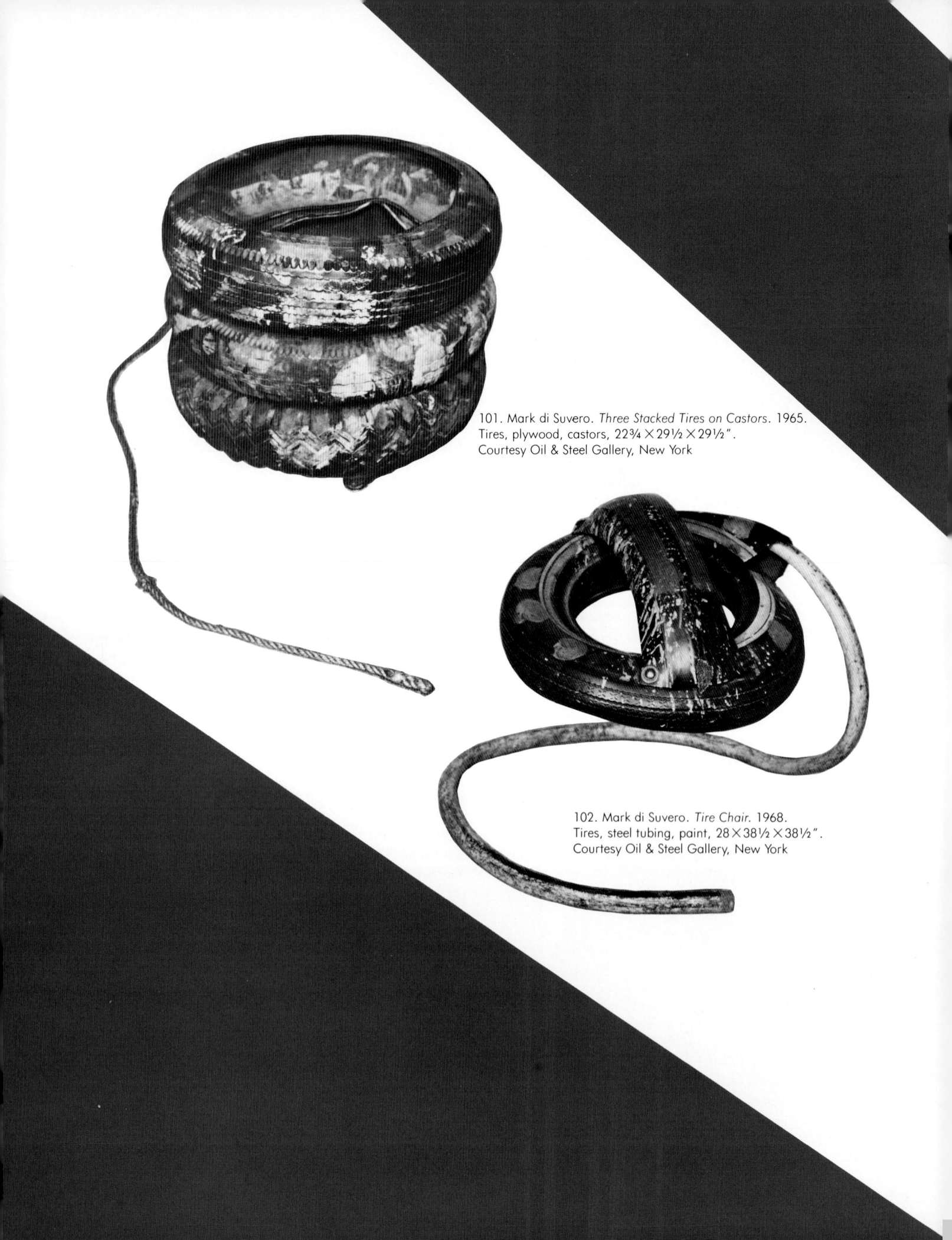

101. Mark di Suvero. *Three Stacked Tires on Castors*. 1965.
Tires, plywood, castors, 22¾ × 29½ × 29½".
Courtesy Oil & Steel Gallery, New York

102. Mark di Suvero. *Tire Chair*. 1968.
Tires, steel tubing, paint, 28 × 38½ × 38½".
Courtesy Oil & Steel Gallery, New York

103. R. M. Fischer. *Flash*. 1980.
Painted steel, office chair parts,
steel wheel and pulley casing, bulbs,
brass rod, aluminum colander,
37 × 26 × 16".
Collection Yves and Francine
Arman, New York

R. M. Fischer

Born in New York, 1947
Lives in New York

I am a sculptor using the lamp in the same way that earlier sculptors used the human form as a vehicle for making an object or an abstraction. The lamp notion demystifies what would simply be an abstract sculpture if it didn't have the ambiguity of functionality. Although the lamps are put together in the tradition of sculptural assembly, an American nuts-and-bolts attitude prevails.

For me the lamp is a loaded object; one comes to it with a whole set of preconceived notions. It has a certain history; the incandescent bulb is a hundred years old, and the lamp is a kind of symbol of our mechanical age. Like others of my generation, I was brought up in a highly visual, pop-oriented culture. I've always been interested in cultural signs and symbols and how we are connected to one another through electronic media, whether it be through film, television, advertising, or printed mass-media. With the power and presence of mass-communication, the artist can no longer isolate himself.

The lamps I make all have this sense of technology, of movies, advertising, fashion, and design all wrapped into one unit. I feel that the strength of my art is that it refers to the mass-culture while retaining its status as high art. Besides making statements about different kinds of styles and sociological references and forcing the viewer to deal with his conditioning, I'm adding the notion that these are animated sculptures that light up, like a film lights up. There is a certain seduction there. I want them to be resolved forms that are both provocative and beautiful and that suggest the future while celebrating the present. I want these objects to wear the ideological fashions that have come to represent our modern world.

104. R. M. Fischer. *Angela*. 1982.

105. R. M. Fischer. *Kensington Arms*. 1982. Wooden table legs, plastic ceiling fixtures and reflectors, metal castings and fittings, aluminum, 72 × 54 × 27". Collection the artist, New York

106. R. M. Fischer. *Twin Falls*. 1980. Stainless steel pan, recycling pump, typewriter stand, galvanized steel ducting, plastic, 36 × 24 × 20". Collection Arthur and Carol Goldberg, New York

107. R. M. Fischer. *Bertha*. 1982. Boiler duct, plumbing pipe, plastic reflectors, crystal, 60 × 38 × 34". Collection the artist, New York

108. James Ganzer. *Pleasure Caddy*. 1982. Palm, wood, Lucite, epoxy, 50 × 38 × 26".
Collection the artist, Los Angeles

Above:
109. James Ganzer. *Palm Dart*. 1982. Wooden bowl, palm, marble, slate, epoxy, 48 × 24 × 18".
Collection Dena Gardner, Los Angeles

Left:
110. James Ganzer. *World Record*. 1982. Palm, Lucite, wooden bowl, aluminum record, epoxy, globe, 72 × 22 × 19".
Collection Stanley and Elyse Grinstein, Los Angeles

James Ganzer

Born in Blue Island, Illinois, 1945
Lives in Venice, California

Before I started painting in 1976, I was a sculptor and had used natural materials like eucalyptus logs and lotuses in my work. I'd resin them and they'd become unnatural natural things; unearthliness is one of the elements I strive to deal with in my work. Though I had avoided making something useful out of the materials, I finally succumbed to using them to make something that was akin to my art but suddenly had function. I like manipulating materials, and I began to incorporate into the furniture all the various materials and found objects I had around.

One windy day back in California I went out and collected all the palm fronds that fell out of the trees. I realized that the stems from the seed pods of the California date palms were harder and denser than other ones, so I took four of them and nailed them around a piece of four-by-four. I didn't try to hide the simplicity of them; they were put together with epoxy and nails. I experimented with all kinds of bases and tops. Then I found a building supplier with broken slate and I bought two palettes of scraps. All the pieces had a relationship to a corner and had broken edges that I found dynamic.

I also have a place in Costa Rica, and that environment has greatly influenced my making of these pieces. In fact the tropical jungle has been the most dramatic change in my life. It's full of information, which I perceive and file in my memory. By grounding myself in that kind of imagery, I can then abstract it as much as I want.

I consider the furniture I make to be my art because it is the sum total of all the parts that go into my understanding of reality and my perceptions of the world. It is all filtered down into these unique objects that I produce.

112. Philip Garner. *Chevrolounge*. 1974.
1954 Chevrolet trunk, upholstery, hardware, 38 × 72 × 36″.
Collection Jeff Cohen, Chicago

113. Philip Garner. *Bunk Easy Chairs.* 1982.
Overstuffed easy chairs, ladder,
steel, wood, hardware, 84 × 36 × 36".
Collection the artist, Los Angeles

Philip Garner

Born in Evanston, Illinois, 1942
Lives in Los Angeles

I am an industrial parasite. It gives me great pleasure to know that a vast system exists to supply me with sophisticated raw materials that I need only modify or place in an unusual context to create my works. I love the products of mass manufacturing. They are the icons of the highest level of cooperation ever achieved in human history. For personal reference purposes I consider society to be at the midpoint of the industrial age. Two hundred years down and two hundred to go. Beyond this my mind is a blank. My work is a tribute to a relatively successful phase in the quest for comfort.

Ever since I first witnessed the introduction of new car models in the showroom, I have always felt the automobile belonged indoors. The transformation of the car into furniture spares vintage vehicular components the abuses of the exterior environment. Practically, the trunk lid when closed keeps the pets off the furniture and when raised creates a cozy canopy effect (with overhead light). Functional taillights mark the horizontal extremities, facilitating entry and egress. The *Chevrolounge* is part of a series of household uses for car parts, including the 1965 Buick *Dashboard Desk* and the 1960 Chrysler front grill *Auto-Style All-Metal Fireplace.*

The bunk easy chairs are a duplex seating module designed to save space, provide a dramatic overview for the topmost occupant, and utilize the upper 50 percent of a room's airspace, which is normally wasted. The "bunk" effect has been restricted to bedroom furniture all too long. Accessories include *Bunk Lamps* (shown), *Bunk Magazine Racks,* and *Bunk Planters.*

The graceful styling and solid construction of a period electric iron need not be lost when the appliance is no longer serviceable in its original task bracket. By recontexting the unit into a lighting fixture, the *Iron Lamp* will bring pleasure for decades to come.

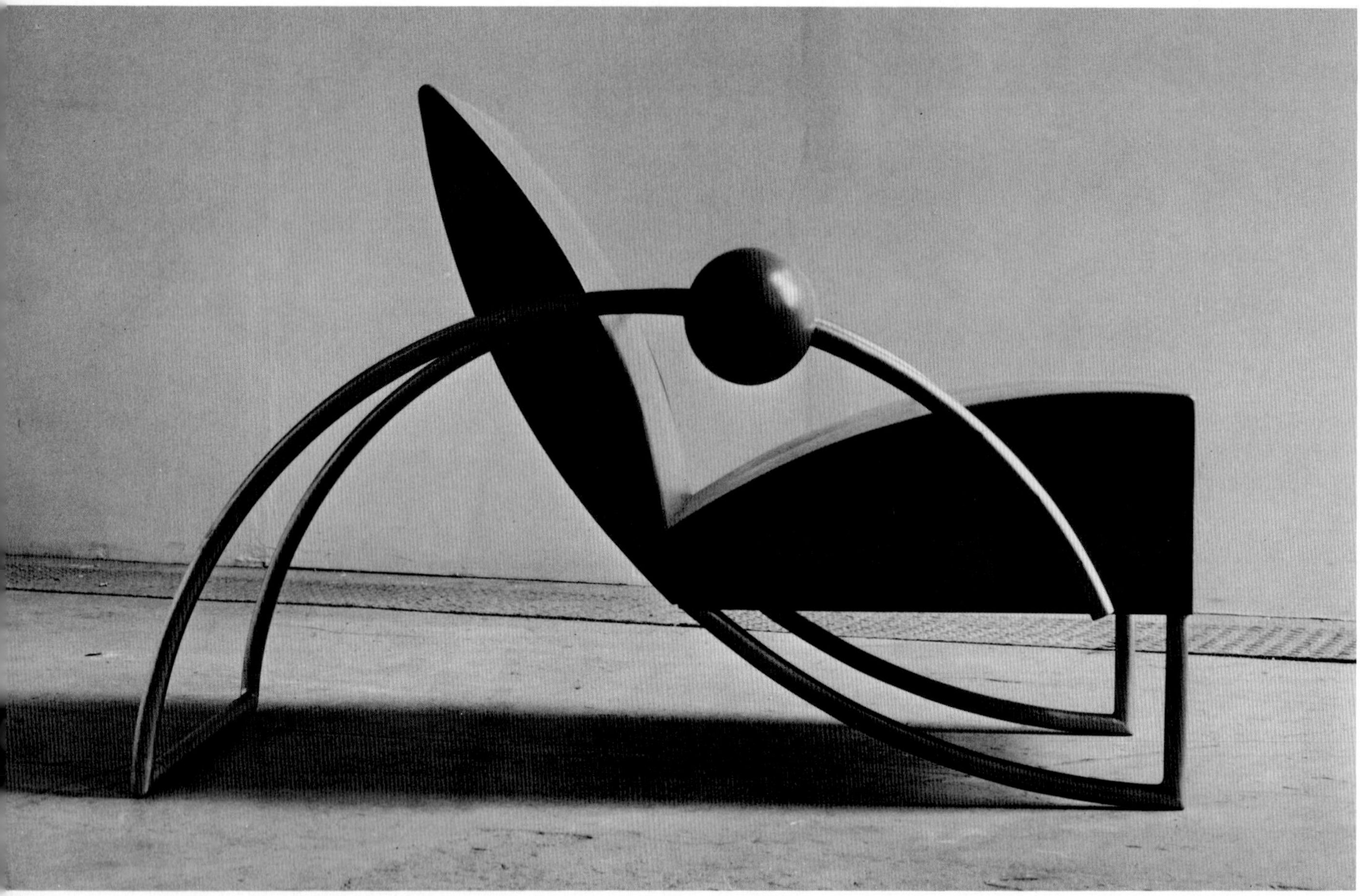

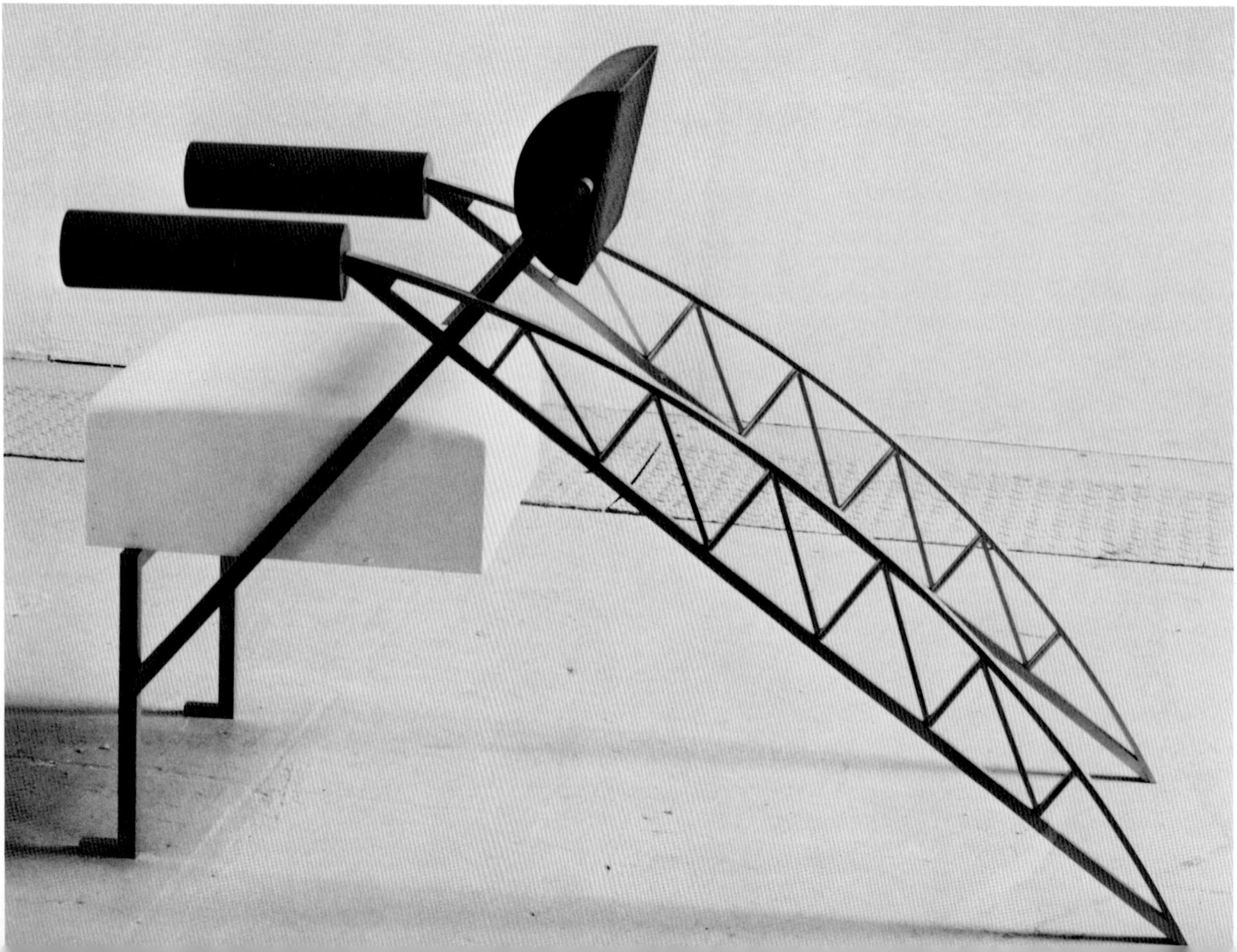

Robert Guillot

Born in Birmingham, Alabama, 1953
Lives in Brooklyn, New York

I call myself a sculptor, but because I make furniture, I have to consider functional aspects. For me the human scale is a good scale for a sculptor. In furniture, scale is largely a question of the relative sizes of the component parts. When a chair is a little larger or smaller than the given standard, it takes on a certain presence. But you can only fluctuate so far, and when I change the scale I'm very conscious of what I'm doing. My sculptural vocabulary is geometry and geometric solids. I'm interested in the circle and the triangle, the sphere and the cone.

I try to start from scratch every time I do something. I come up with an idea and whatever material suits that idea is what I use. I bounce back and forth from one extreme to the other. Once I'll do an open framework, then I'll make something very dense and solid. I go from truth to the materials to its opposite. Sometimes the upholstery looks crisp and hard but it isn't, or sometimes you can see just how the iron is cast and poured. I can't put my finger on why I'm doing this, but what happens in pushing the elements around is what keeps me doing it. I don't make something because it will do this and that. Something is glimpsed obliquely which does not jibe with what you know. For an artist, what he already knows is the least interesting thing he can do.

115. Robert Guillot.
Untitled (Triangle/Circle Lamp). 1980.
Aluminum, fluorescent
and incandescent bulbs, 20 × 13 × 3".
Multiples/Marian Goodman Gallery,
New York

Opposite, top:
116. Robert Guillot. *Untitled (Pink Chair).* 1980.
Stainless steel tubing, vinyl, 29 × 25 × 47".
Multiples/Marian Goodman Gallery, New York

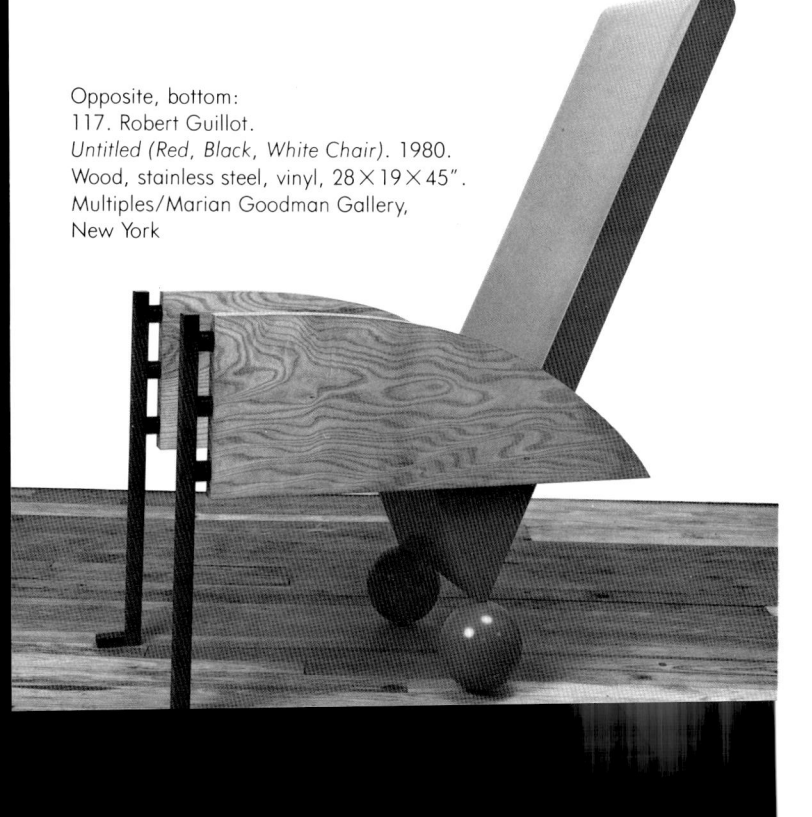

Opposite, bottom:
117. Robert Guillot.
Untitled (Red, Black, White Chair). 1980.
Wood, stainless steel, vinyl, 28 × 19 × 45".
Multiples/Marian Goodman Gallery,
New York

118. Robert Guillot. *Untitled (Green Chair).* 1979–80.
Wood, cast iron, paint, vinyl, 51 × 20 × 41".
Multiples/Marian Goodman Gallery, New York

I consider myself a sculptor of functional and nonfunctional objects. About fifteen years ago I started making furniture for myself out of necessity, and in 1972 I began making it for others.

When I set out to make my nonfunctional pieces, the only requirements are my own; the sky's the limit. With the functional pieces, the requirements, whether simple or complicated, make me stretch a little further and discover things about myself and my capabilities.

I'm a craftsman in one sense, but I like the fact that I have resources of other people's expertise. It would be very limiting to feel that every element in one of my works had to be done by me. Rather, craftsmanship is a conceptual part of the art. It is symbolic of different periods in history and different civilizations that have influenced me. For example, the way I use gold leaf recalls an esoteric technique of the fourteenth century. My use of anodized aluminum and fiberglass refers to universally accepted techniques of the twentieth century. Historical references are apparent in the forms as well. In *Dunhill* the form is very elemental, which is a contemporary ideal, but there is also a reference to a Chippendale drop-leaf table.

One of the shapes that intrigues me the most is the full circle. It implies completeness and takes in the concept of Gestalt. The floating, gravityless quality in my work implies freedom. Suggested motion, roundness of form, softness of surface, and the combination of materials are recurring themes and concerns common to all my work.

119. Peter Gutkin. *Three Columns*. 1982.
Carved glass, varnished and painted wood,
height: 15"; diameter: 48".
Collection the artist, San Francisco

Peter Gutkin

Born in Brooklyn, New York, 1944
Lives in San Francisco

120. Peter Gutkin. *Dunhill*. 1982.
Varnished bird's-eye maple,
granite, 15 × 60 × 30".
Collection Auguste Wheeler,
Mill Valley, California

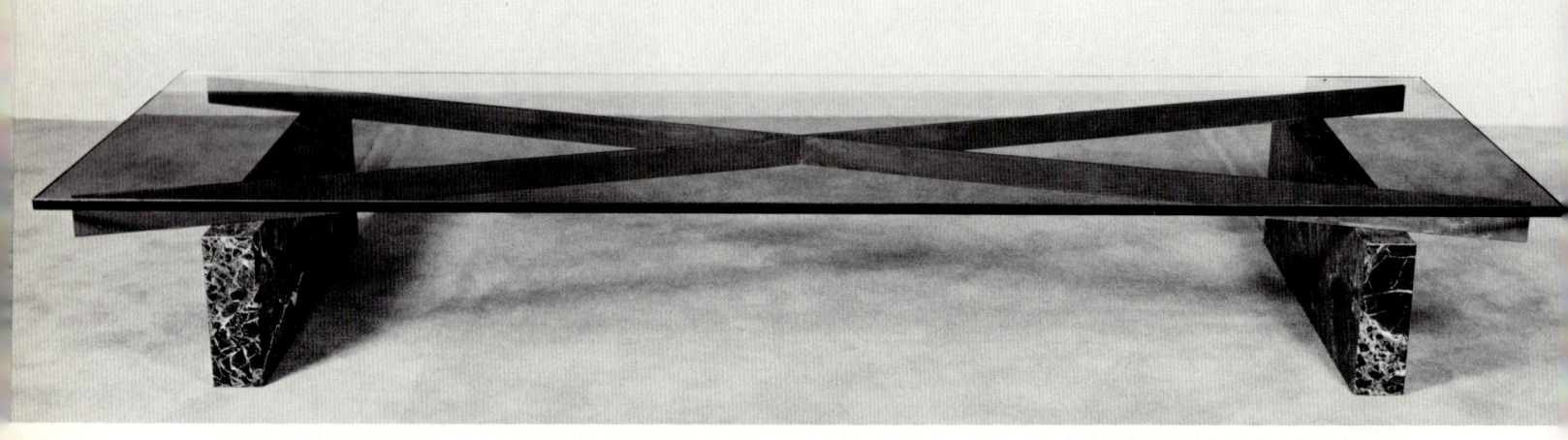

121. Glenn Heim. *Montifiore Table*. 1981. Glass, copper, marble, 15×96×30". Collection Stephen Montifiore, New York

122. Glenn Heim. *Long Bench/Table*. 1978. White pine, 18×112×16". Collection the artist, New York

Glenn Heim

Born in Bellevue, Iowa, 1939
Lives in New York

My furniture has a professional context: I have an industrial design background and have worked for years in furniture design and architecture as well. However I also paint, because there are certain kinds of imaginative content that I can't deal with in design. Sometimes my painting is affected by my design work in that I deal with it as an object to be displayed—designing it and engineering the structure and frame—more than someone who is just a painter. It's a strange kind of mixture. It has to do with my interest in context, which is an important conceptual concern in everything I do.

My most successful way of working with furniture is to begin with the entire space qualitatively. Doing the whole environment is what inspires me. First I orchestrate the space, build it well and logically. Once the sense of space is right I begin work on the smaller parts, building up to the whole gradually, in layers. I like to build the furniture with attention to raw materials, delicacy of detail, and proportion, relating it all to its environment. It should be quiet and anonymous and function well.

People have commented that my work is Japanese in sensibility. Perhaps that's because I'm a horizontal person. I admire the strong visual integration of the Japanese, but I've always thought of myself as Western. For me Shaker furniture is the paradigm with its subtlety, directness of design solution, quality of materials, and perfection of scale.

I've found that furniture works well as a metaphor for other structures, and I'm using it to practice more complex and larger ones. I'm not totally aware of my next step, but I'll go where it looks exciting.

84

George Herms

Born in Woodland, California, 1935
Lives in Orange, California

My first works were true labors of love: gifts for birthdays, anniversaries, celebrations, visual occasional verse. Later they ended up in museums and galleries as works of art. My background as an artist has come from beachcombing. I use found objects in my work and see the process as an alchemical one in which I take what has been discarded and breathe new life into it.

My clocks are called *Time Reliefs*. I used to call on the phone to get the correct time because my studio didn't have a clock. One day the phone just kept ringing—no answer. This brought to mind a clock cliché from my youth: "That bum, I wouldn't give him the time of day!" Thus I went out and purchased parts to make a clock and made my first one. The clocks are nothing more than my continuing assemblage works with the addition of clock hands. There are never any numbers on the clocks, and they are all set at different times, which has a disturbing effect on the viewers. The movement of the hands continually changes the composition. The quality movements are battery-operated and last about a year, so there is a final place where the hands end up (chance).

The *TLK Coffee Table* was a commission based on sculpture, wherein I covered surfaces with stained coffee filters. The filters take on a Japanese landscape quality. The wordplay was also a factor in the conception of the "coffee table."

My description of the works is "furniture for the soul." Our need for beauty is as real as hunger and thirst. The optimum aspiration would be to make all aspects of daily life works of art. Richard Serra said: "If it's functional, it's not art." Give me one year and I'll turn any outdoor sculpture into a sundial.

Upper left:
123. George Herms. *Trine Time on Birdcage Stand*. 1980.
Wooden easel, metal, paint, clock, clock assemblage, 52 × 16 × 13".
Collection Ruth Schaffner, Santa Barbara, California

125. James Hong. *Karnak*. Bookcases. 1979.
Wood, glass, lacquer, electrical, telephone, and cable outlets, 60×16".
Art et Industrie, New York

126. James Hong. *Tropic of Cancer*. Table/desk. 1981.
Glass, concrete, wood, lacquer, 30×84×36".
Art et Industrie, New York

James Hong

Born in Vallejo, California, 1948
Lives in New York

127. James Hong. *Wavelength*. Wall lamps. 1982.
Tubular aluminum, lacquer, quartz halogen bulbs, lengths: 48–79".
Art et Industrie, New York

I did most of these pieces in an eight-month period. Doing an intense body of work in this way enables one to confront oneself and see what the work is all about.

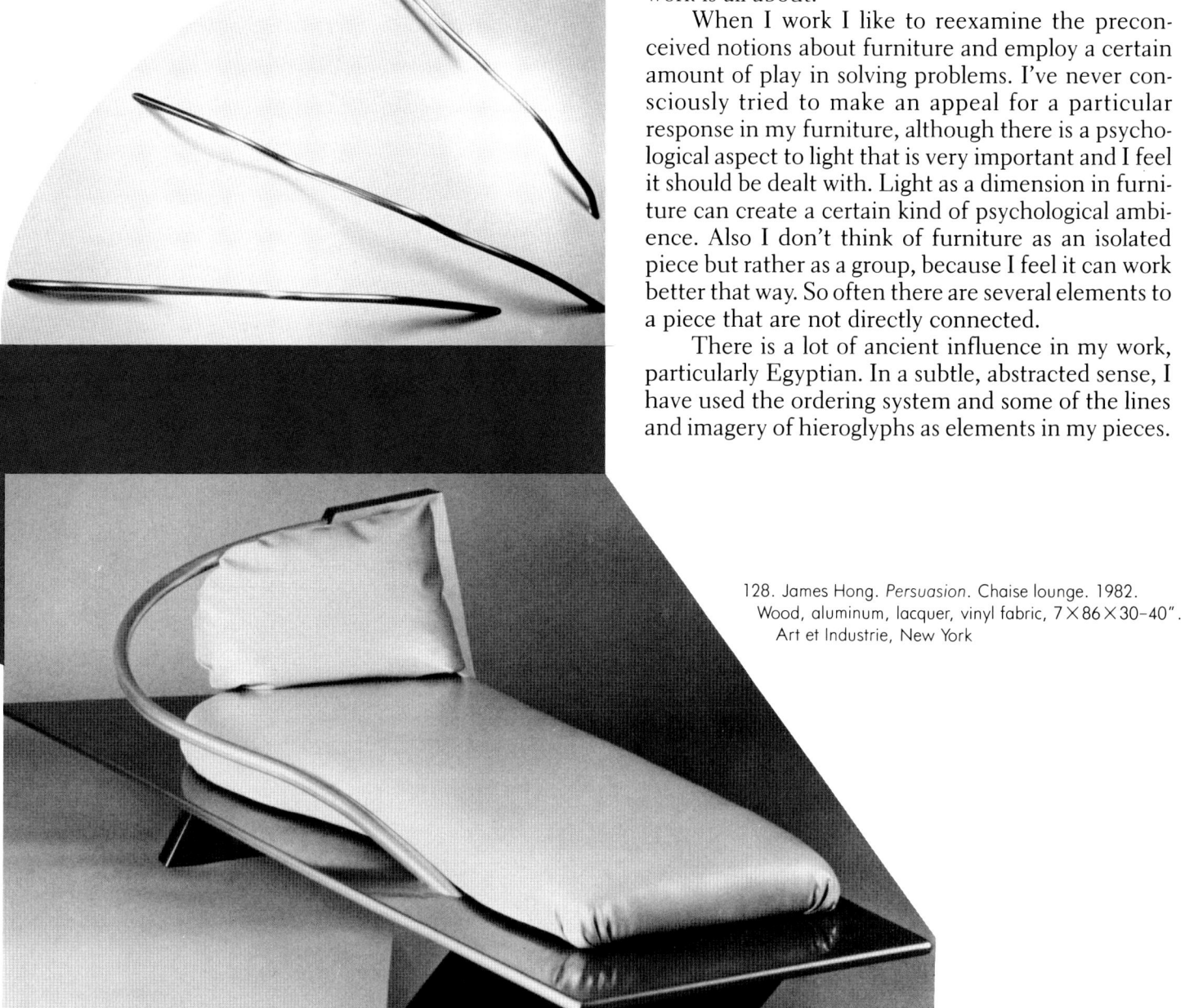

When I work I like to reexamine the preconceived notions about furniture and employ a certain amount of play in solving problems. I've never consciously tried to make an appeal for a particular response in my furniture, although there is a psychological aspect to light that is very important and I feel it should be dealt with. Light as a dimension in furniture can create a certain kind of psychological ambience. Also I don't think of furniture as an isolated piece but rather as a group, because I feel it can work better that way. So often there are several elements to a piece that are not directly connected.

There is a lot of ancient influence in my work, particularly Egyptian. In a subtle, abstracted sense, I have used the ordering system and some of the lines and imagery of hieroglyphs as elements in my pieces.

128. James Hong. *Persuasion*. Chaise lounge. 1982.
Wood, aluminum, lacquer, vinyl fabric, 7 × 86 × 30–40".
Art et Industrie, New York

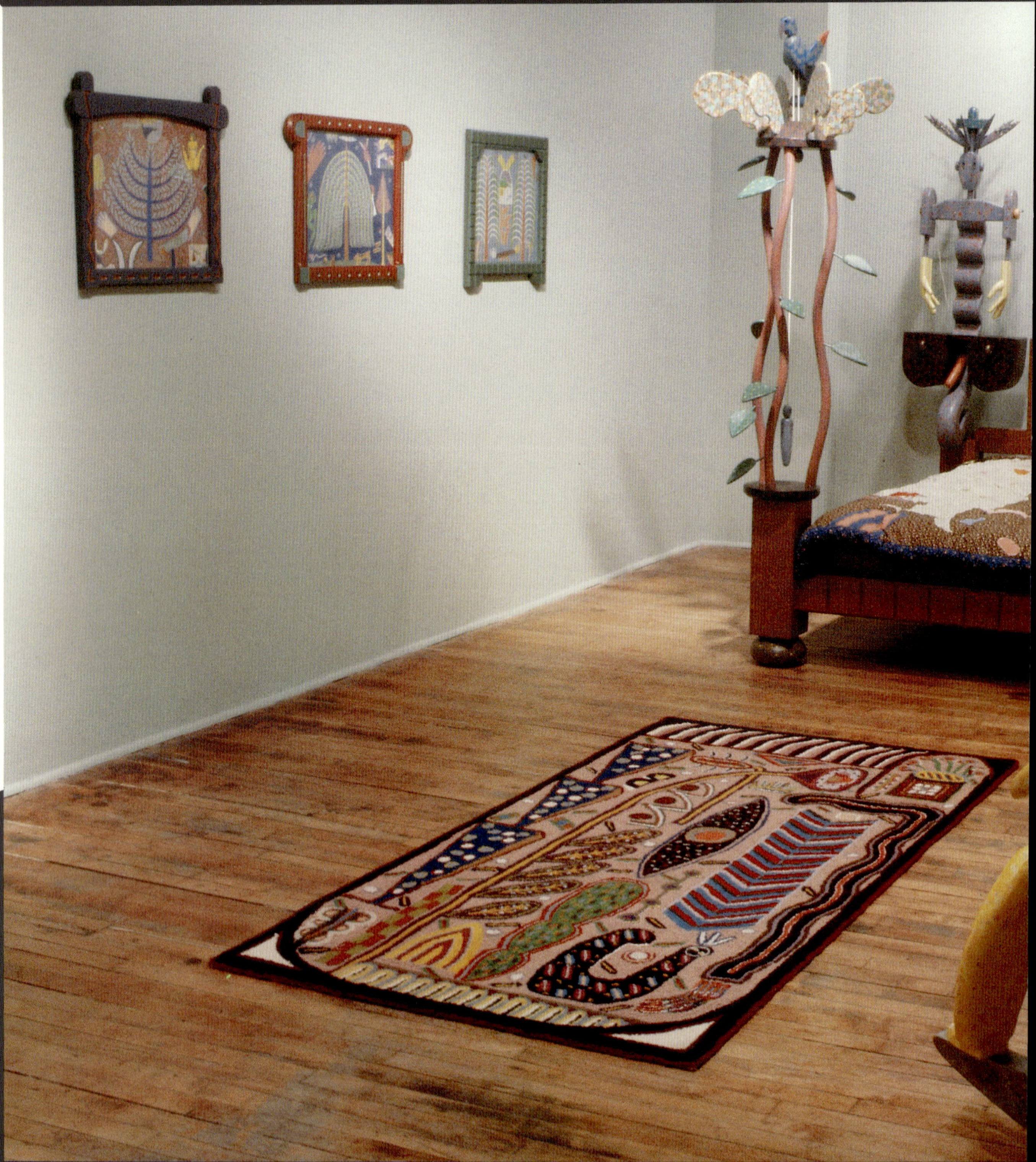

Klindt Houlberg

Born in Chicago, 1937
Lives in Chicago

I wandered into furniture making as a result of two trips to Nigeria in 1969 and 1973. West African art is expressed through functional things—through weavings, carvings, everyday objects. The people there simply don't make art for art's sake, and I began to see art through their eyes. The experience gave me confidence about a certain directness of image that I had been thinking about before I went, and I began to incorporate flora, fauna, and figures into my iconography.

I see my work as flirting with the line between function and fantasy. All my rugs, quilts, and furniture have a certain humor to them and a kind of imagery that is almost lyrical or poetic. I think of each piece as a functional structure, although the pieces are not for everyday use or for mass production. I make them usable, but they are art.

129. Klindt Houlberg. *Delux Sweet*. 1980.
Installation includes: *Heart of Art*. Four-poster bed. 1980.
Polychromed wood, 78 × 64 × 84";
Lap Time. 1977. Polychromed wood, 62½ × 34 × 33".
Collection Monique Knowlton, Illinois.

Polychromed wood, hooked rugs, gouache on paper in painted frames, appliqué quilt, 12 × 18'.
Courtesy the artist, Chicago

130. David Ireland. *South China Chair.* 1979. Pelembang cane, paint, 42 × 48 × 48". *Lamp.* 1982. Concrete, copper tubing, miscellaneous electrical parts, height: 50". Leah Levy Gallery, San Francisco

David Ireland

Born in Bellingham, Washington, 1930
Lives in San Francisco

I conceived the design for the chairs about twelve years ago. The idea was to take a traditional overstuffed chair and translate it into another material. It could have been marble or something else, but in this instance I was working in the Orient and decided to make the chairs out of rattan. I wanted them to be theatrical and larger than life. That exaggeration does something to the space and to the sitter as well. When I showed them in a gallery, I did two things. I made quite an issue of building up the surface in a variety of colors, though the final layer is gray, and I called them paintings—because painting in its traditional sense is an illusion of reality—and I also showed them illuminated by spotlights in the darkened gallery. One saw them initially from behind because I wanted the idea of object-form to emerge at the same time.

In the case of the lamps I simply wanted to throw materials together and see if they didn't connect some way. I wanted to go as directly as possible from electricity to light.

Before making furniture I had been a printmaker and painter and had started to sense the tyranny of materials and traditional format. I also felt that to go anyplace one had to sacrifice security. Since the home is the strongest symbol of that, I began with the old Victorian house I had bought to live in. First I challenged the security of the home by violating the architectural order. I took molding off the walls and stripped it selectively of other elements. At the same time I treated the cleaning of the house as an exploration of a relic, gathering brooms, string, rubber bands, those trivial things I found throughout the house that are used incrementally and mark time in a way. These things were evidence of the history of social systems. My coming here added to those layers of information that I uncovered and "stabilized." They were here, left their mark, and I tacked on. The chairs and lamps, though mine, relate to those kinds of notions about my house.

Dakota Jackson

Born in New York, 1949
Lives in New York

I come from a long line of magicians. I worked professionally until I was twenty-two, billing myself as a "miracle worker." Then I moved into the art scene and staged what I called "miracles." What interested me more than the performances themselves was the fantastical historic line or mythology generated by these events.

The furniture was an outgrowth of building magic illusions for magicians. I was always involved in two things: the mechanics that facilitated the illusion and the choreography of the illusion, the interplay of the objects. So as a designer I began as a magician/choreographer. Rather than someone simply working three-dimensionally, I was working experientially. In incorporating hidden compartments, movement, and the unexpected into the pieces, I tried to create a sense of anthropomorphic intelligence that was competitive with anyone who came up against it.

The early concepts were developed very literally. The *Standing Bar* refers to an abstract version of the different boxes a magician might use. There was never the notion of its being only open or closed, just in different states. More interest and surprise are created as one disrupts its static state and exposes the internal elements. The piece completely explodes.

The concepts of the later pieces have more subtlety expressed in potential energy and movement, in the visual tension of minimal support and counterbalance of elements, and in the precision behind the way a piece operates and holds together. I like the idea of pushing the technology and quality of workmanship and detail to its limit.

Standing Bar (side view).

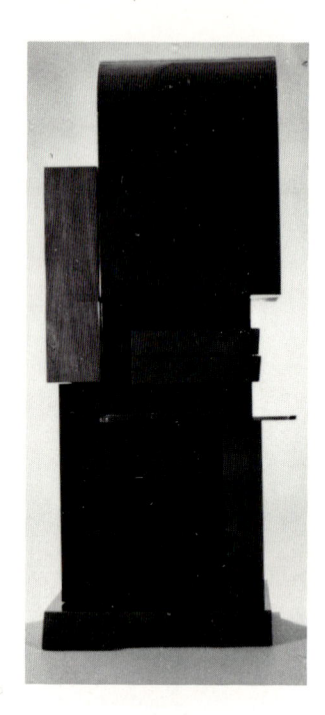

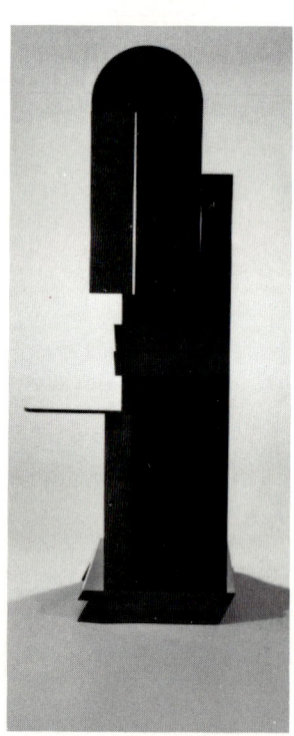

131. Dakota Jackson. *Standing Bar.* 1979. Edition of 15. Mahogany, lacquer, glass, 72 × 31 × 27" (closed); 72 × 70 × 27" (open). Collection Roselee Goldberg, New York

132. Dakota Jackson. *Fan Cocktail Table*. 1982. Travertine marble, brass, glass, 35 × 48 × 16". Collection the artist, Long Island City, New York

133. Dakota Jackson. *Flag Cocktail Table*. 1982. Travertine marble, glass, 26 × 26 × 14". Collection the artist, Long Island City, New York

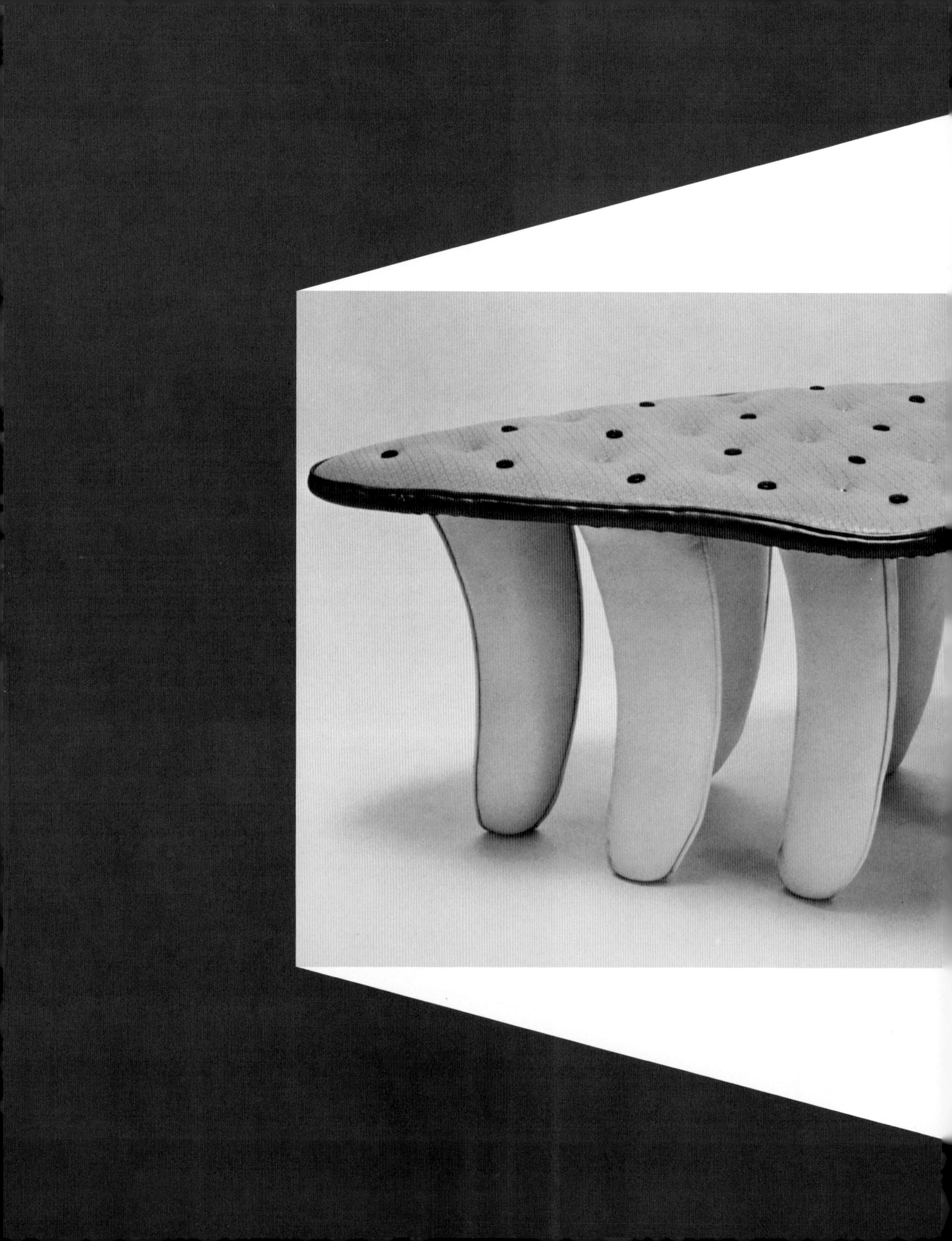

Elizabeth Browning Jackson

Born in Providence, Rhode Island, 1948
Lives in New York and Newport, Rhode Island

I have worked in a lot of different mediums and done environmental sculpture, textiles, and design. My grandfather was an architect, my grandmother a founding member of the American Institute of Design, my mother was in the Bauhaus, and my father's family had textile mills in Rhode Island. With my background it was very stimulating to bring everything together in the furniture.

Before I started the furniture I had been doing airbrushed paintings on metal, so making tables and shelves was just a change of form. Combining metals, industrial paints, vinyls, and metallic acrylic fabrics pushes the pieces into the future; I'd like my work to be space age. I also want the pieces to be fun and crazy, not intimidating, and I draw from nature because I like the furniture to have the feeling of animation.

Too often the excitement of art is left in the artist's studio, limiting the public's response to that of a spectator rather than a participant. By designing furniture and rugs, I want to make art less sacred so that people can not only view it, but can sit on it, walk on it, eat off of it, deal with it directly. In that way they can become part of the excitement too.

134. Elizabeth Browning Jackson. *Feather Teeth.*
Cushioned stool. 1982.
Vinyl fabric, wood, 18×30".
Art et Industrie, New York

135. Elizabeth Browning Jackson.
Projection. Low table. 1982.
Steel, lacquer, 14×24×55".
Art et Industrie, New York

136. Elizabeth Browning Jackson.
Recent Landing. Chair. 1982.
Vinyl fabric, metal, rubber, fiberglass,
38×30×18".
Art et Industrie, New York

137. Elizabeth Browning Jackson.
Installation. 1982.
Includes table: cushioned vinyl, steel, 14×48×16";
rug: acrylic deep pile, multichemical dyes, 120×36".
Art et Industrie, New York

Tom Jenkins

Born in Kansas City, Missouri, 1943
Lives in Santa Monica, California

My father came out of the Ozarks, and I grew up with tales about surviving entirely off the land and about hillbillies and their particular kind of ingenuity. I respect that folklore and find it exciting. The obsession and energy of folk artists somehow gets into their objects and makes them magical. I find in them new aspects of object-making that I'd never thought of before.

I'm fascinated by how things work and I teach myself and explore things like spinning tops and solar-generated electricity in my work. I was interested in learning about sound and in sounds that I could physically make myself. I jumped into a whole tradition, like one would jump into painting. First I started with the basic principles of instruments and reconstructed them for myself. At the same time I was doing carpentry and finding out how hand tools worked. I looked upon the tools as sculpture in themselves. So I decided to build the table and chair entirely out of hand tools, keeping in the sculpture tradition and carving geometric planes from scratch.

The table is a basic soundboard with hollow legs and a hollow space underneath the top. I played with the different sounds I could make, pounding on it, bouncing things on it, stretching a wire across it. I had some stone strikers, brushes, a rubber mallet, a bridge, and a treadle to adjust the tension of the wire. Then I built some steam pieces that could make sound on their own and I clamped those on. I stored these things in the chair. In performances I'd start with the bare table and pull things out of the chair and demonstrate how they worked, like the mad scientist. Toward the end the sound would just continue on its own. The table became a kinetic sculpture that created movement and sound whose fluctuations and pitch were determined by physical laws and were independent of me.

138. Tom Jenkins. *Sound Table.* 1977.
Alder, mahogany, oak, rubber, glass,
music wire, metal, wax, 34 × 27 × 48".
Collection the artist, Santa
Monica, California

Neil Jenney

Born in Torrington, Connecticut, 1945
Lives in New York

Furniture is not really an integral part of my work, although I think about it a lot. It's like doodling, a break from the philosophic profundities of art. This table came as a sudden flash in my mind, and I made it because it was dissimilar to all the tables I had seen. It has harmony and aesthetic viability. It makes you want to go over and have lunch on it. But for me a piece of furniture is simply a three-dimensional object. It has no image of social import, no timeless content. Furniture is not art.

139. Neil Jenney. *Staggered Table*. 1976. Edition of 200. Painted wood, Formica, 28½ × 61 × 42". Multiples/Marian Goodman Gallery, New York

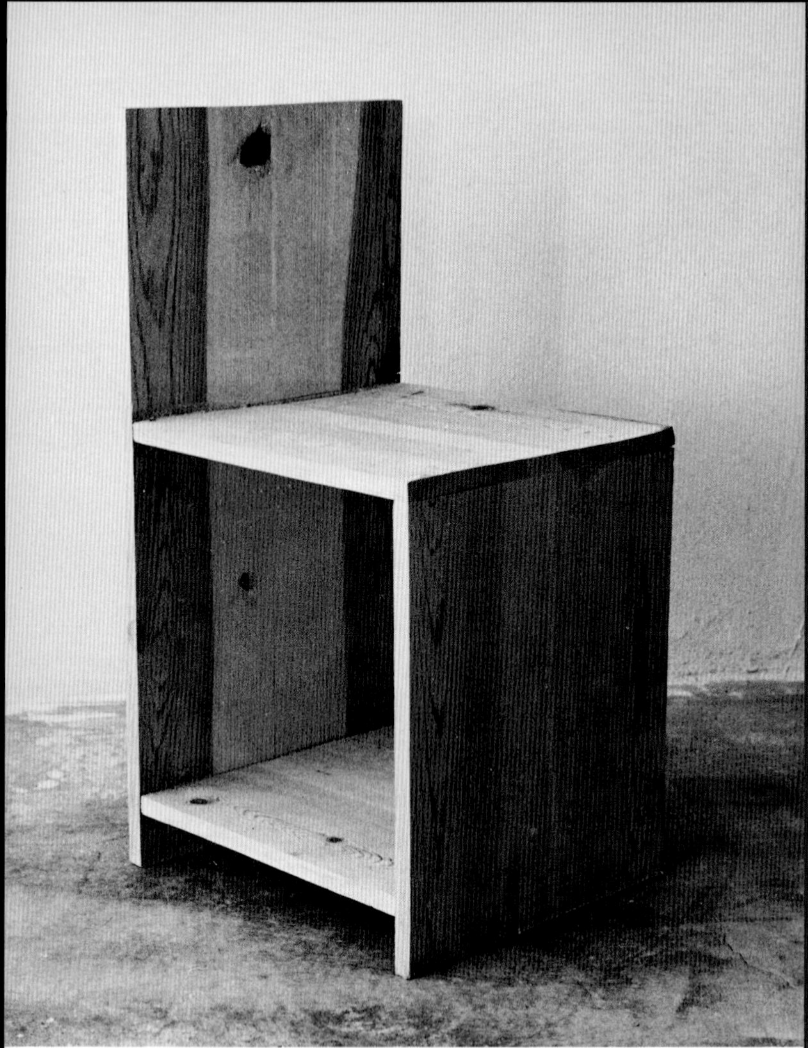

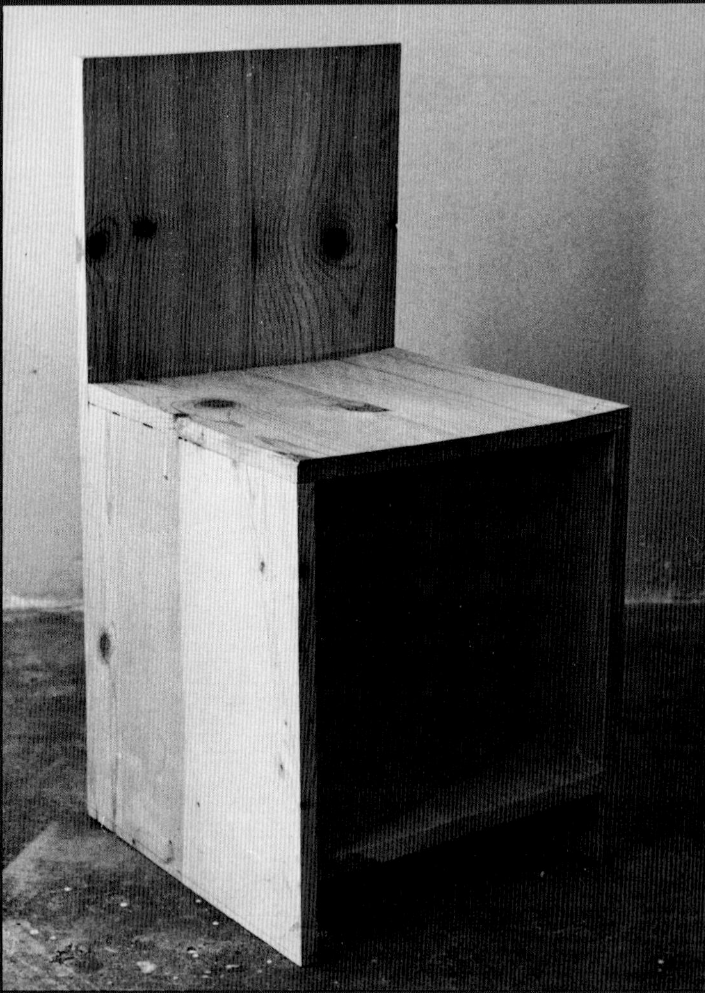

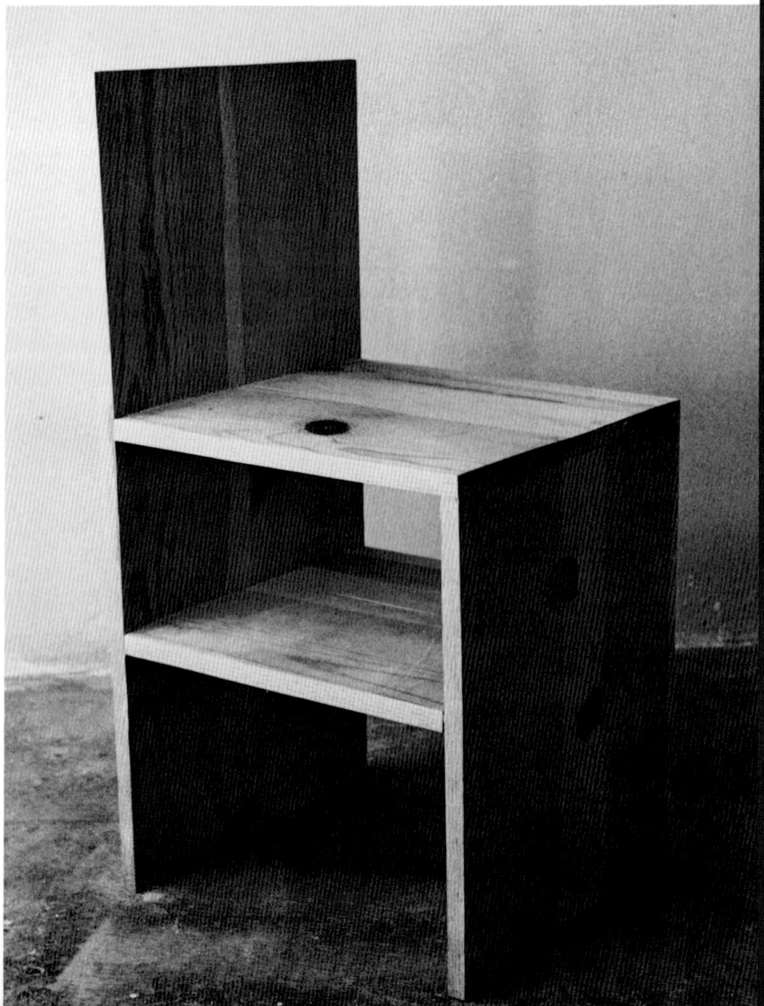

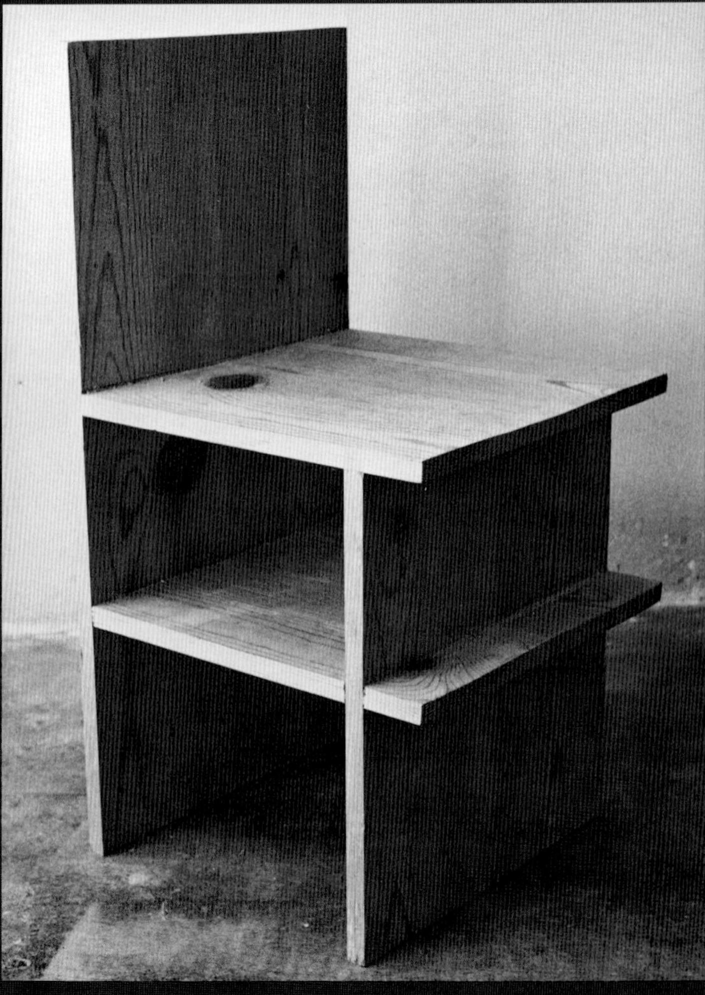

Donald Judd

Born in Excelsior Springs, Missouri, 1928
Lives in West Texas

Furniture is important to me. I've always reworked the space I lived in and have often made furniture for it. Perhaps the first things I made—about fifteen years ago—that were really furniture were some metal chairs and a table. Now I'm making a limited edition of chairs, a desk, and a table. I started making them in Texas in 1978.

Since there's no decent furniture for sale in the small town where I live, it's necessary to make it. So far I haven't made furniture for anyone else, only for myself. The idea of making furniture to sell is very recent. In Texas the furniture is based on the width of the wood. We use pine, and the construction, by Celedonio Mediano, is simple and straightforward. In New York we use birch or maple, and the construction is extremely sophisticated. The main thing about the chairs is the vertical planks that make up the backs. The fronts and the sides are just different ideas. I spent quite a lot of time trying to make the proportions even, one to two, which I like, or two to three, and so forth.

Much of the harmony in an environment is in its proportions. It's an old idea in architecture, but I don't think people now are very concerned about it. When I fix up or make buildings, their proportions are very important to me. The buildings are primarily for the installation of art. I have a lot of my own work, and I want it installed properly. Then I have quite a bit of other people's work, and it takes a lot of space. I'm very serious about this, and that's the main reason why I keep getting more space.

I've spent quite a bit of time on the furniture, so I don't consider it frivolous. But I am an artist, and therefore the art is more important. I make a big distinction between the art and the furniture and architecture. I'm careful about taking ideas from art and placing them in another context.

140. Donald Judd. *Six Side Chairs.* 1979.
Pine, each 30 × 15 × 15".
Collection the artist, Texas

141. Annie Kelly. *Veracruz*. Three-panel screen. 1983.
Oil on canvas, 60 × 66".
Collection the artist, Los Angeles

Annie Kelly

Born in Adelaide, Australia, 1954
Lives in Los Angeles

Fixing my house has given me somewhere to put all the decorative ideas I've been storing up. As a painter I've spent years working with color, shape, and composition, and decoration incorporates all those elements. Using my house as a workshop in this way has really loosened me up and changed my work. For one thing I've learned to work with materials that used to intimidate me, like stucco and wood.

At one point I wanted to do a big painting, and there was the structural problem of support. I bought a saw and turned it into a screen. My paintings—frontal, architectural orderings of receding planes—were discarded in favor of the theatrical three-dimensional illusion that working on the ground suggested. I tried to change the subject matter according to the new format and experiment with landscape. I could do anything I wanted with the back of the screen.

The wall hangings and rugs are really abstract compositions and totally different from my paintings. I love what Sonia Delaunay did on fabrics, and it was interesting to see if I could duplicate that. Since the hangings and rugs are decorative, I felt I could get away with borrowing from anything stylistically, and experiment.

A lot of the design ideas come from places I've been in, like Italy and Mexico. Though the influences filter through in a fuzzy way, I don't care because it is the personal fantasy that is important. I'm living in what used to be Mexico and that influence is strong here, so I like drawing on Mexican culture and carrying that aesthetic through in my own way. The house is a workshop and my decorative ideas feed into the art and the art into the decoration.

142. Annie Kelly. *Installation* (artist's home). 1982.
Three-panel screen, reverse shown: oil on canvas, Masonite, 60 × 66"; two-panel screen, reverse shown: oil on canvas, Masonite, 60 × 44"; *Diana*: three-panel screen, acrylic on canvas, particle board, 28 × 25"; wall hanging: acrylic on canvas, 108 × 33". Collection the artist, Los Angeles

Whit Kent

Born in Sault Ste. Marie, Michigan, 1913
Lives in New Jersey

I'm an artist. I haven't done anything but paint. I had a store and got a little bored, so I started making flat plaques out of pine. Pine doesn't have a very interesting surface, so I decided to paint them. Then I decided that to make the plaques look round, I should paint them to look round. Then I thought that if I'm going to make them look round, I should carve them round. That's the way it started about six years ago.

I taught myself about wood. I discovered very early on that carpenters really don't know the answers, and that's when I stopped asking anybody how to do it. I just shuffle on through till I get where I want. It takes longer that way, and because you have a feeling there's an easier way, it's like sweating blood.

Pine is the cheapest and the easiest wood to work with. I'm interested in a medium that I can use that displays what I want to express. If I get into hardwood, I'm just working on a piece of hard wood and not getting my ideas across in a hurry. I'm too old; I have to do things in a hurry.

I've done hands a lot. Hands are very important because what can you do without them? I don't know what I'd do without mine.

This country is built on buying something useful rather than decorative. I think it's sort of built into our natures. Back in colonial times one didn't have anything that sat around just being beautiful, it had to be useful as well.

I think art can be found everywhere. This separation of things annoys me. If you can do a painting, you certainly can do an etching or make a piece of furniture. It's all art. That's my idea anyway.

143. Whit Kent. *Fish Chest.* 1980.
Pinewood painted, varnished,
and waxed, 14 × 16 × 10".
Courtesy Julie: Artisans' Gallery, New York

144. Whit Kent.
Screen with Three Figures. 1979.
Pinewood painted, varnished, and waxed,
66 × 48 × 3".
Collection Mr. and Mrs. Jack Stievelman,
New York

145. Whit Kent. *Hands Chest.* 1979.
Pinewood painted, varnished,
and waxed, 32 × 21 × 16".
Courtesy Julie: Artisans' Gallery, New York

Thomas Lanigan-Schmidt

Born in Elizabeth, New Jersey, 1948
Lives in New York

146. Thomas Lanigan-Schmidt.
Daytime/Nite Light (A Solitary Drinker). 1973.
Mixed media, 40½ × 24½ × 15".
Courtesy Holly Solomon Gallery, New York

I am a practicing Greek Orthodox, but I think like a lapsed Catholic. I grew up in a small, ethnic, working-class town, and what I do relates to my background and is also in conflict with the situation I find myself in now.

I want my pieces to be devotional and make people feel good. I use inexpensive materials that you can get at the five-and-ten: Saran wrap, candy wrappers, wire glitter, foil, Magic Markers. I want them to be beautiful, so I try to make them sparkle. Glitter and sparkle have a theological basis. It's supposed to be the energy of God's grace. God is always called the Light, and that is the basis for it in Orthodox ritual. It's distorted sometimes when the gold and glitter become something worth money and money becomes the symbol instead. Part of the message of my art is that beauty can be deceiving and everything we value can fall apart, so my materials are intentionally ephemeral.

The *Daytime/Night Light (A Solitary Drinker)* has someone "sitting pretty" on top, and the whole environment she's sitting on is encrusted with bugs and flies and held up at the bottom by other people. In the center are a small shot glass and a pretty pitcher. It's about the D.T.'s and a lot of other things as well. We are all sitting pretty in a sense because a lot of other people are doing works and suffering for our sake. That's very unfair, so all the prettiness is like a mask.

The kinds of things I do always have very dim bulbs in them, so you can't really sit next to them and read a book. They're just art pieces that have a light in them. It's alright to call them lamps, but if you want to use them as functional lamps, you have to face this fact.

147. Sol LeWitt.
Coffee Table. 1980.
Wood, glass, 16 × 48 × 48".
Multiples/Marian Goodman Gallery,
New York

Sol LeWitt

Born in Hartford, Connecticut, 1928
Lives in New York

I do wall drawings and geometric figures; my ideas pertain to order and things of that sort. I make things for myself that I need because I feel I can design them better and make them cheaper than I could buy them. My tables have grids in them and are very uncomplicated. The grid makes decisions for you; it's a way of evening out space. I made a table fifteen years ago and the grid was painted on the wooden top: white lines on a gray table. This one is kind of a follow-up to that. The proportions were determined by what I needed for the space here. I've made things progressively for my loft. I think one naturally makes one's environment if one stays in a place long enough.

148. Roy Lichtenstein. *Modern Table*. 1970.
Brass, dark glass, 17¾ × 58 × 58".
Courtesy Leo Castelli Gallery, New York

Roy Lichtenstein

Born in New York, 1923
Lives in Southampton, New York

I'm interested in contradictions, excesses of style, subjects that have a great deal of meaning before I use them, like a Matisse or the pyramids. A cartoon that is an extreme of style, an entablature, a brushstroke, practically everything I've done has inherent contradictions and absurdities.

Doing furniture was considered frivolous in the seventies, when everyone was concerned with getting to the basis of art. I think artists shied away from furniture making because they were afraid to be associated with it in some way.

My table was part of the sculpture I was doing at the time, and I made it because we wanted a table. I was working with glass, brass, and some marble, and doing sculptures that really derived from handrails in movie theaters. My influences then were Minimal art and Art Deco, the latter I thought had a Minimal, geometric quality. When I was doing my railings, practically nobody was involved with Art Deco, but almost immediately afterward (having nothing to do, I'm sure, with what I was doing), there seemed to be a tremendous interest in it. I had seen some buildings that were Art Deco and the style looked like humorous Minimal art to me, Cubism for the home. It didn't have a serious purpose to my mind; or maybe it was too serious. It was so intellectual and funny, with three repeated curves or a cube that diminished in size. It seemed to be the opposite of Abstract Expressionism and Minimal art, but very much like "Pop" in certain ways. I wanted my sculptures to refer to Art Deco without really looking like it.

I made three tables and live with one of them. I went about it in exactly the same way I did the sculpture, so although I had to think about their use, I really can't see any important difference.

Susan Linnell

Born in Taft, California, 1940
Lives in Albuquerque, New Mexico

From time to time I do things tangential to my painting. These pieces were play, a game. I've used cardboard for a long time to mock up forms in my paintings, but the furniture fulfills a fantasy of exploring another dimension in a completely free way. Cardboard has what I want from a material. It's flexible, light, quick, disposable, and I can cut all the shapes freehand. The immediacy of it is very important to me. I "dressed" an old table and chair with the cardboard forms, and then to make it more permanent I had it coated by a fiberglass fabricator. This gave the cardboard an interesting texture before I painted it and kept the pieces light enough to move around. The weight issue is important because I rearrange my furniture about once a week, and it frustrates me if I'm unable to move things by myself.

In my paintings I'm after a sense of animation, movement, and theatricality. That the furniture is vaguely cartoonlike is no accident since it's an element in my work. It's a constant struggle to keep my art at the quality and level that I want, but in these pieces I didn't even think about it.

I use this furniture in my house. The pieces are more like living things than other furniture because they have a persona about them, which designed furniture doesn't. Although I like extremely severe environments, my own has always tended to become pretty animated.

Kathryn Loye

Born in Oklahoma City, Oklahoma, 1953
Lives in Los Angeles

This chair developed out of shapes that have religious connotations. While I was exploring and excavating local junkyards for metal shapes for my aluminum paintings, I kept seeing beautiful linear pieces of metal that looked like three-dimensional line drawings. Some were mechanical parts, others were old chair parts. I bought them and began thinking of them as sculptural color drawings and fantasy furniture with functional pretenses.

I collect architecturally inspired furniture and beautifully designed anonymous objects. I've always wanted my possessions to have aesthetic value. It seemed logical to me to combine art ideas with functional design.

150. Kathryn Loye. *Pseudo-Religious Chair.* 1982.
Found mixed metal, oil enamel, 65 × 29 × 12".
Courtesy Norman Mauskopf, Whiteley Gallery, Los Angeles

149. Susan Linnell. *Screen, Table, Chair.* 1982.
Pine, fiberglass, acrylic, screen: 53 × 73";
table: 29 × 72 × 42"; chair: 45 × 22 × 21".
Collection the artist, Albuquerque, New Mexico

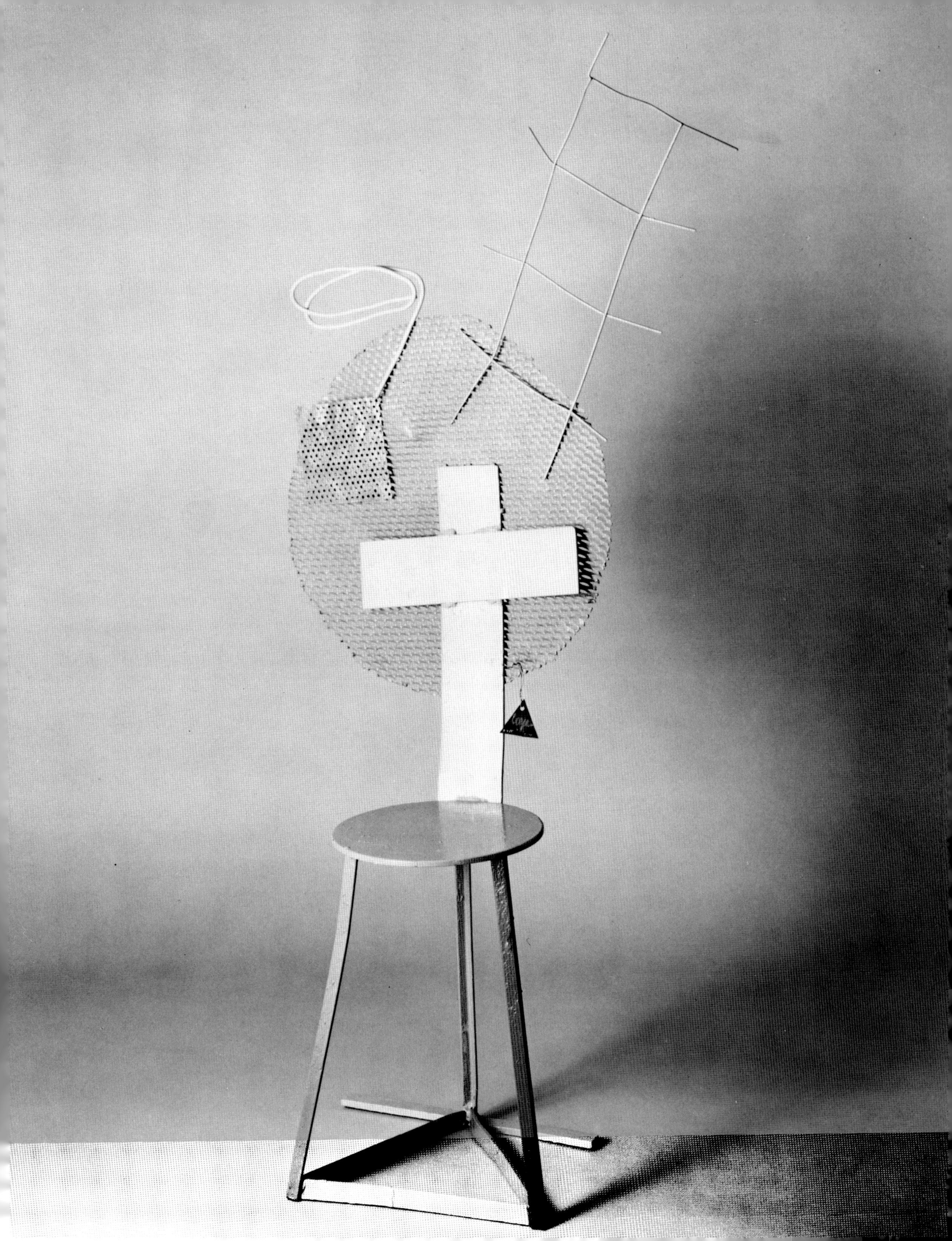

151. Kim MacConnel. *Painting, Chair, Lamp.
Da Loop* (painting).1979. Acrylic on cotton,
8'4"×9'10"; *Chair.* 1978. Found chair, paint,
45×22×22"; *Sports Lamp.* 1978. Plastic bowling
pin, ball, golf club, oar, metal standing ashtray,
height: 60". Collection the artist, Encinitas, California

Kim MacConnel

Born in Oklahoma City, Oklahoma, 1946
Lives in Encinitas, California

I had been involved in collecting and researching flat-woven textiles. My graduate thesis in 1971 had to do with decoration. In the Middle Ages textiles were used to make the environments livable. It seemed to me that the tent of a primitive goatherd in some outlying region in the Middle East had visually richer, more varied notions of decoration than the environment of someone living in the twentieth century. I felt then, and still do, that a lot of intellectual visual skills had been lost. My ideas were heightened by Minimalism, which I viewed as cold. I wanted to drop back to a premodernist time, to a different mind-set. I was particularly interested in transposing to the twentieth century notions of chinoiserie, ornamentation, and exoticism in an eighteenth-century salon sense. This idea of decoration seemed like a subject worth playing around with, so I set about trying to cram as much of it into my work as possible.

"Decoration" and "applied art" were pejorative terms in the early 1970s, less than pure art. I wanted to utilize the term "decoration" for what it meant, without placing judgment on it, as a tool to play out that idea. It has been said that decoration and patterning have no intellectual content, but formalist painting doesn't either, and yet the same criteria can be applied. Both are concerned with picture plane, flatness, surface, and gesture. Formalists and Pattern painters use the same grid and just fill it in different ways; the overlays are what make it intellectually interesting. I tried to stick to certain formalist definitions and at the same time utilize complexity in my work. I was drawing from everything from Oriental carpets, African stuff, and Picasso to doodads I found on the street. I took the surface image and applied it to other things like furniture and clothes. The context and environment of my art give it definition and intellectual content.

I'm not compulsive about it; I don't paint on every single thing in my environment. It's the rhythm, variation, and the utilization of pause and space that are interesting. Pattern as repetition is not. The other concerns are what take it beyond the basically boring.

152. Kim MacConnel. *Couch, End Table, Lamp.*
Curved Pink Couch. 1982. Upholstered sofa, acrylic, 33 × 92 × 41".
Harlequin End Table. 1982. Wood table, acrylic, 31½ × 30 × 21".
Lamp. 1982. Found lamp, acrylic, 35 × 10".
Courtesy Alberta College of Art Gallery, Calgary, Alberta, Canada

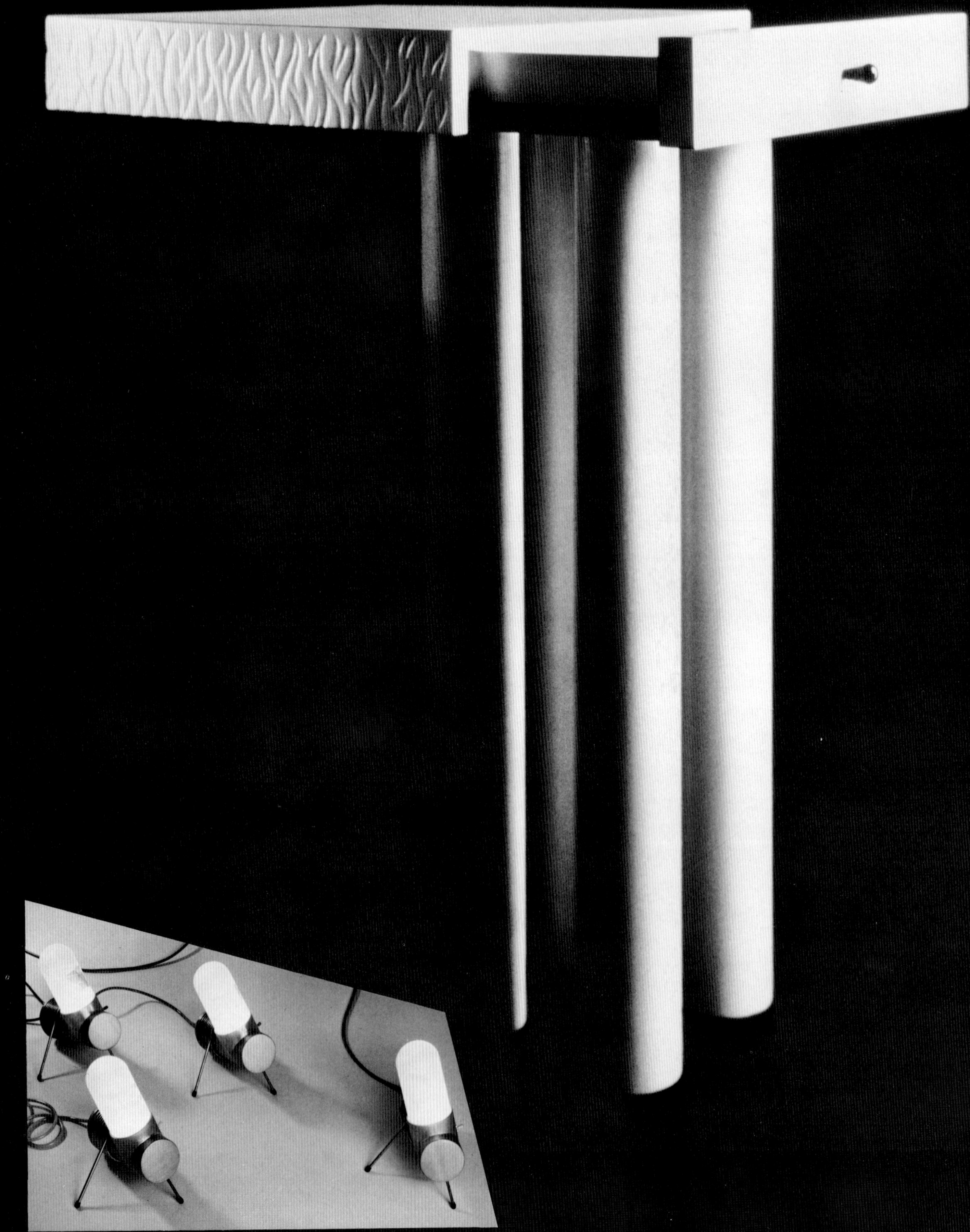

Opposite, left:
153. Main & Main. *Cloud Prop.*
Floating drawer. 1982.
Wood, stainless steel,
plastic laminates, 72 × 32 × 32".
Fabricator: General Specialties,
New York.
Art et Industrie, New York

Opposite, insert:
154. Main & Main. *Moondogs.* Lamp. 1982.
Aluminum, glass, 14 × 3½ × 10".
Art et Industrie, New York

Main & Main

Terence Main
Born in Indianapolis, Indiana, 1954
Lives in New York

Laura Main
Born in Crawfordsville, Indiana, 1953
Lives in New York

Before furniture we had been making sculpture, models, and small-scale environments. We both feel that information is very important and we accept it as a function. Besides providing exciting images, we hope our furniture provides exciting information that can change and elaborate your life and open your imagination. The objects represent the statements we want to make and the stances we want to take with regard to the world we live in.

Our furniture is a joint pursuit. It's preschool play and we are having fun. We talk incessantly as we work, draw a lot, make models, and pass the objects back and forth. We engage different industries, different fabrication techniques, and different materials. We're completely open and don't let our limitations bother us; in fact we deliberately experiment and switch to a new idea once we've learned something.

All our pieces tend to be future-oriented rather than images from the past. If there is a retrieval of past notions, we deliberately try to muffle them and take them somewhere else. Our furniture makes a conscious effort to fight conditioning and throw off conventional behavior so you'll wake up and feel. We want to aggressively distort the rectilinear qualities that are so much a part of the International Style. We like the fact that things are wavy and not at perfect right angles. They're harmoniously perfect because they're made by man and not the machine. We feel our pieces are playful and sophisticated in the sense of a Miró painting. Though craftsmanship is important, we're trying to make our new pieces as free, light, energetic, and carefree as possible.

155. Main & Main. *Mothra.* Chair. 1983.
Wood, steel, leather, brass, lacquer, 49 × 17 × 17".
Fabricator: General Specialties, New York.
Art et Industrie, New York

Opposite, center:
156. Main & Main. *Triatron*. Lamp. 1982.
Shades: hand-molded, hand-tinted fiberglass;
base: slip-cast molded ceramic; 18 × 10 × 13".
Art et Industrie, New York

157. Main & Main.
Queen Anne, Queen Anne.
Chair. 1982.
Wood, velvet, lacquer, 44 × 27 × 16".
Fabricators: Hudson Frame and General Specialties, New York.
Art et Industrie, New York

Opposite, far right:
158. Main & Main, Tom Nicholson, and Eric Chan.
Ribbon. Chaise lounge. 1981.
Wood, lacquer, plastic, and metal laminates,
72 × 32 × 32".
Art et Industrie, New York

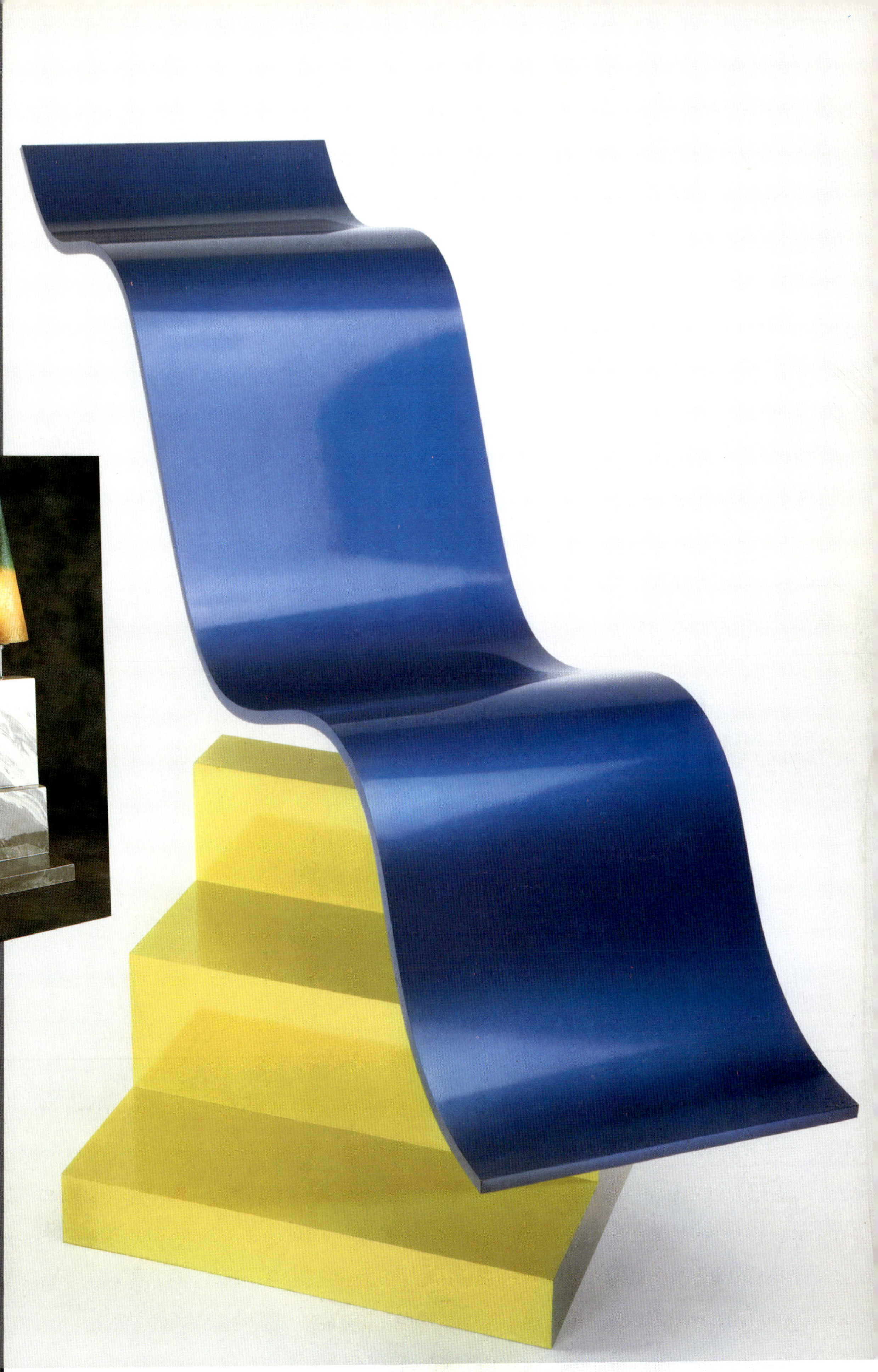
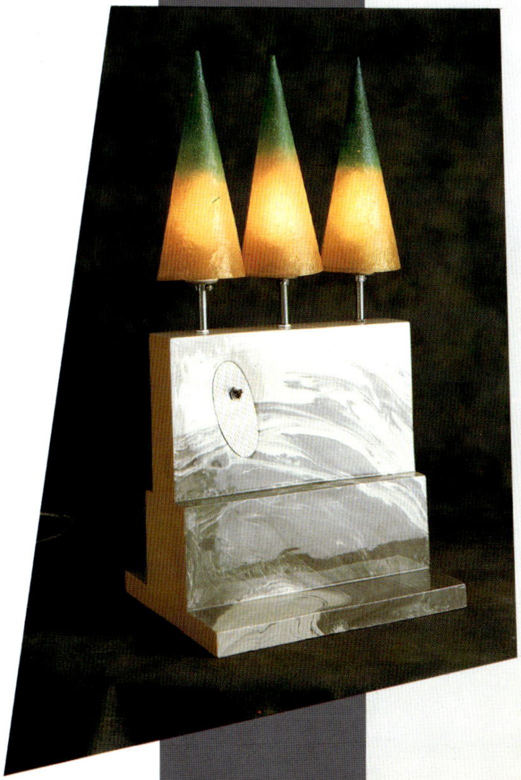

159. Wendy Maruyama. *Striped Pinto.* 1981.
Polychromed plywood, glass,
15×48×24".
Collection the artist,
Smithville, Tennessee

160. Wendy Maruyama.
I-15 to Vegas. 1982.
Veneers, plywood, neon,
glazing points, paint, 28×11×5".
Courtesy Convergence Gallery, New York

Wendy Maruyama

Born in La Junta, Colorado, 1952
Lives in Smithville, Tennessee

I consider myself an artist who makes furniture or furniture-related objects. Although I was trained as a woodworker/cabinetmaker, this bit of training is a small facet of what I do. I have tried going beyond traditional woodworking—which for me is very oppressive—by exaggerating traditional furniture forms. Recently the terms "usable art" and "sculptural furniture" have been used. My work is furniture more or less, but there is a bias that divides craft and art. I choose to be in between and make the objects without being concerned with craft or the traditional requirements of furniture.

There are many sculptors who use furniture imagery, and theirs is considered a legitimate art form. I would like to do the same thing with my furniture pieces and not be berated for it by craftspeople or artists. When I see a painting or a drawing that I respond to, I try to understand what it is that I like and introduce that quality into my work. Before, I didn't think that was possible; painting was painting. But now I don't hesitate to use color and have sculptural ideas. Often the function of my pieces is secondary or sometimes it is not apparent at all.

I see furniture as an archetypal object that can also be expressive of the times. Furniture is capable of setting a certain mood and reflecting common ideals in our lives. I think furniture can have the same impact as a painting or a piece of sculpture.

161. Wendy Maruyama. *Red Wedges*. 1981.
Wood, steel, paint, epoxy, tape,
36 × 18 × 18".
Courtesy Convergence Gallery, New York

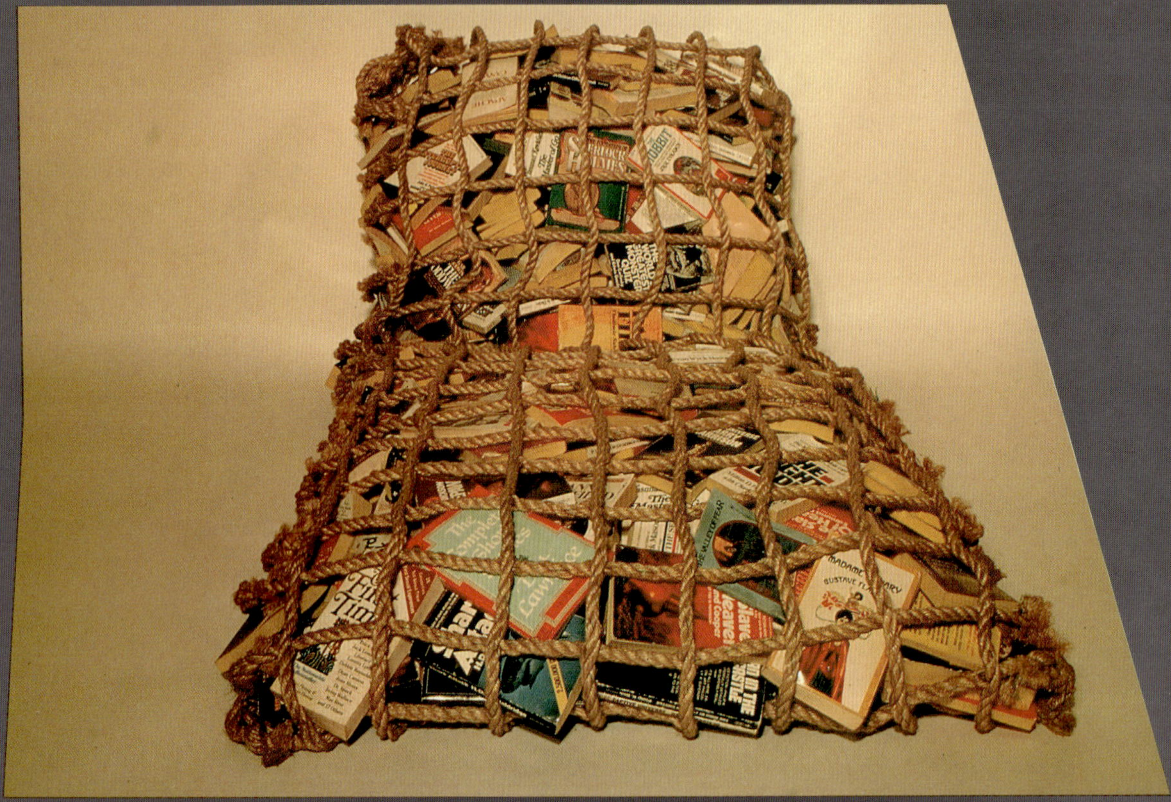

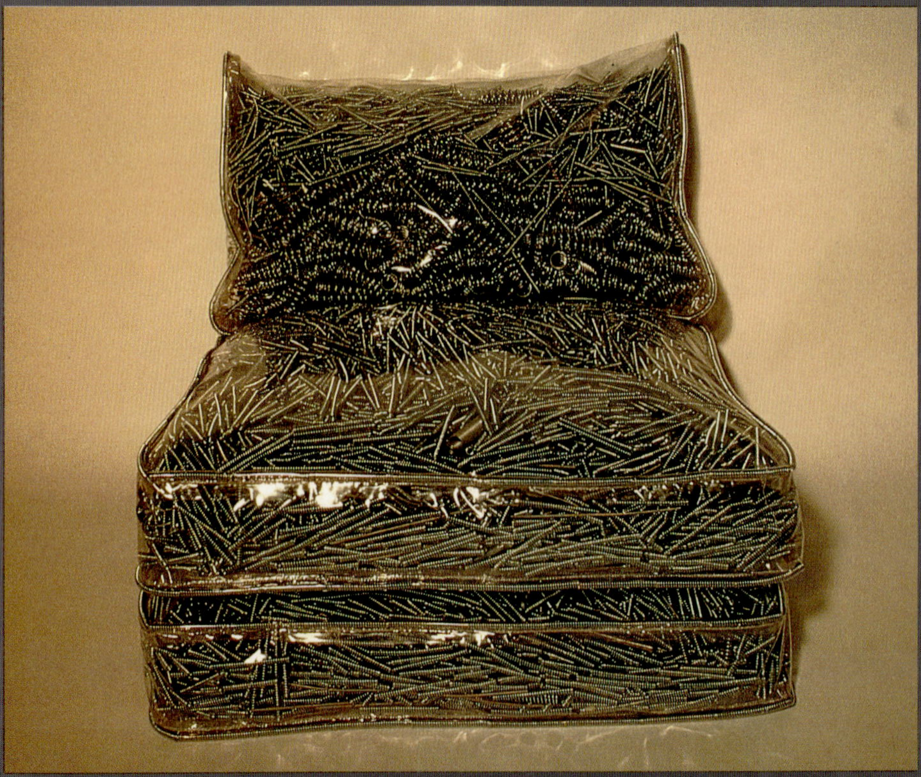

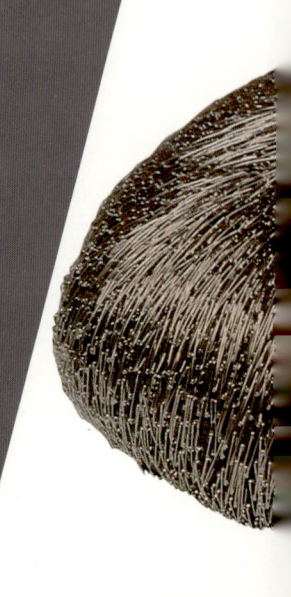

Richard Mauro

Born in Brooklyn, New York, 1946
Lives in Brooklyn

What I think I'm after in terms of art is an "antisymbol" for furniture design, the opposite of what people consider it to be. I want to resensitize the cognitive aspects of sitting down and to shake up the habitual reflexes by violating preconceived notions. I want form and function to oppose each other aggressively. I want to invoke a challenge.

My pieces are meant to create a dialogue between the spectator and the object by stimulating in the interaction, not only multisensoral perceptions, but a reevaluation of our society's limitations and expectations as well. To some extent my work is in retaliation to the waste and corruption of industry. Thus the components are standard, familiar objects dislocated from their reference to our technological past and present. Furniture is an area where art and technology are closely interlaced. I want to make people aware of the limitations of technology and of the unlimited possibilities of art, where man can emerge from behind the shadow of the machine.

Dali said: "A chair must serve to cause the proud, ornamental, intimidating, and quantified specter of a period to spring forth instantly." My work attempts to mold the visible and invisible iconographies of our society by volumizing banal, disregarded, discarded objects and enabling them to discharge an ornamental and practical function uncaged from the conventional grammar of style.

Opposite, above:
162. Richard Mauro. *Library Chair.* 1978.
Cargo netting, five hundred paperback books,
30 × 50 × 36".
Collection Michelle Stone, New York

Opposite, below:
163. Richard Mauro. *1828 Chair.* 1979.
Vinyl fabric, sixty-seven pounds of assorted springs,
28 × 36 × 36".
Collection the artist, New York

164. Richard Mauro. *Safety Pin Amoeba.* 1977.
Surplus army blanket, textile waste filling,
one thousand #3 safety pins, 15 × 84 × 36".
Collection the artist, New York

165. Richard Mauro. *Discus.* 1978.
Aluminized nylon outer cover,
eighteen-ounce canvas inner bag,
chipped and broken cafeteria plates,
height: 12"; diameter: 46". Collection the artist, New York

166. Judy Kensley McKie. *Bench with Horses.*
Carved mahogany, 17½ × 60 × 27".
Courtesy Museum of Fine Arts, Boston.
Purchased through funds provided by
the National Endowment for the Arts
and the Deborah M. Noonan Foundation

167. Judy Kensley McKie. *Couch with Gazelles.* 1978.
Carved poplar, 27 × 82 × 35".
Private collection, Los Angeles

Judy Kensley McKie

Born in Boston, Massachusetts, 1944
Lives in Cambridge, Massachusetts

I got into furniture partly as a reaction against painting. I couldn't justify making things that simply hung on the wall. At the same time I had a bare apartment to furnish, and I began making the functional pieces I needed. I gradually became addicted to furniture making, and now I can't stop.

While I was learning to build, my designs were pared down and straightforward. Designing became automatic, and to challenge myself I returned to the creative process that included visual imagery. I wanted the pieces to come alive, so using animal forms seemed a logical way to animate what I made. I think I purposely avoid imagery that is too specific because I don't want to reveal everything right away. I want the animals to be magical and mysterious.

There is never one source for an individual piece. I'm constantly looking at Pre-Columbian, African, Indian, aboriginal, early Egyptian, and Greek art and artifacts, and these influence the way I design and think about shapes. I find the interpretation of reality in this art the most direct and honest. There is also a lot of sculptural thinking in the making of a piece so the entire thing reads as one idea. The craftsmanship is very much integrated in the work, but I don't think it is more important than the idea.

Art needn't be a painting in a gallery; it can be a sign on a wall; it can be a piece of furniture. If the image and the idea are powerful, then it's art.

168. Judy Kensley McKie. *Glass Top Side Table.* 1981.
Painted birch, 30 × 52 × 18".
Courtesy Sherley Koteen Associates, Massachusetts

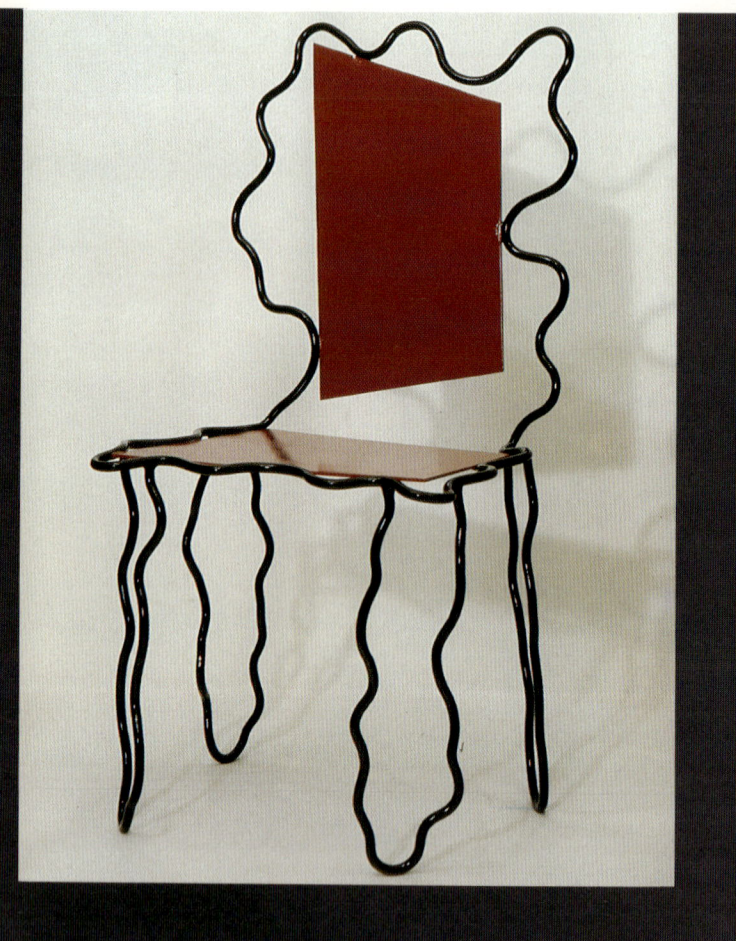

Upper left:
169. Howard Meister. *P-Strut*. Chair. 1982.
Painted steel, 39 × 21 × 22".
Art et Industrie, New York

Lower left:
170. Howard Meister. *Nothing Continues to Happen*. 1981.
Painted hardwood, 37 × 16 × 17".
Art et Industrie, New York

Below:
171. Howard Meister. *Learning Her Lie*. Chair. 1982.
Painted steel, 40 × 16 × 17½".
Art et Industrie, New York

Howard Meister

Born in New York, 1953
Lives in New York

I was dissatisfied with drawing and photography because I found them too specific. I wanted to make broader, more general statements about humanity and to find something that was an abstraction for the human body.... I'm not interested in lamps or cars or typewriters, so when I hit on the idea of using chairs, it seemed like the magic item. They are like human anatomy in division, they hold you, and they're ubiquitous.

I formulated the basic form for the chair so it would be instantly recognizable. Then I started doing things to the chairs to say this could happen to you or any physical thing that happens to exist. When I began I knew virtually nothing about carpentry and friends helped me. As I learned the techniques I started to do the major part of the work myself and enjoy doing it, although the idea behind the piece remains my motivation. Now I get the best of all three worlds: my drawings can be what they want to be, my photography continues, and the chair allows me the freedom to be more abstract and general.

You don't always perceive a chair as art; it exists in your living room, so the message slips subliminally by your guard. My chairs are about the regimentation of modern architecture and design, urban violence and danger, the effects of time and natural forces on matter, and mythology, among other things. That's why I like working with chairs: you can go very far when you start with one little common ground. The chair is all the common ground I need.

172. Howard Meister. *Juvenile Offender*. Chair. 1982.
Steel, lacquer, 44 × 28 × 17½".
Art et Industrie, New York

Susan Michod

Born in Toledo, Ohio, 1945
Lives in Chicago

173. Susan Michod. *Dinoflage Camousaur.* 1981. Acrylic on canvas, wood, plastic, steel, 72 × 120 × 48". Susan Caldwell Gallery, New York, and Jan Cicero Gallery, Chicago

In my earlier work my sources were textiles and all kinds of weaving. Although I worked with patterns in my paintings, I wasn't interested in ordinary decoration, but in how the paintings affected things around them. As I stamped the patterns out randomly, I began to see images and to feel they were more and more important.

Later I found several chairs that were unusual, and the more I looked at them, the more they suggested other things. I like the idea of finding objects, seeing something in them, and transforming them to bring that out.

Art should change your perception of the world, and when it becomes environmental, the impact becomes more direct. In *Dinoflage Camousaur* the painting is almost a stage set for the objects that are camouflaged in it. The paint comes off the canvas and onto the wall and objects. It is important that the paintings be unstretched because the thinness on the wall accentuates the fact that painting is illusion and the object is an object. Although the painting defines the objects and one's reference to them changes when the image relationship is discovered, there is bound to be a disjunctive leap between the two.

I like the chairs to be usable, but since I'm after the image of them, I don't know how to draw the line. I would recommend them only as an occasional place to sit.

Libby Mitchell

Born in Philadelphia, 1928
Lives in Hermosa Beach, California, and Seal Harbor, Maine

I relate very much to nomadic peoples, and weaving is a form common to them all. There's a beauty in the continuity of it, and I love to use their methods.

My furniture began ten years ago with an academic interest in California Indian basketry. I studied all kinds of basketry wherever I could, and I learned traditional caning and seating methods in France and England. As my methods got tighter I combined techniques and made looser pieces as well, using other natural fibers that I came upon where I live in Maine and California.

For my pieces I look for antique chair frames that are familiar to everybody, like a Chippendale chair, and take their beautiful lines and do my own thing with them in a material completely unrelated to the original style. I did the couch and chair entirely myself out of huge bunches of pine needles and draecena palm. They're very strong.

My painting is not affected by this activity. If you're a painter, painting is always the most important part of your life. Nothing can change that. But working with plant fibers gives me a feeling for sculpture, and I may even get away from making furniture and make objects with them. I don't like it when people ask me to make something. I have to be inspired. I don't want to be a furniture-maker, but I don't mind being an artist who makes furniture.

174. Libby Mitchell.
Loveseat and Armchair. 1981.
Wood, pine needles,
New Zealand flax,
yucca, hemp,
armchair: 36 × 20 × 20";
loveseat: 36 × 28 × 20".
Collection Mr. and Mrs.
Robert Courtney,
Hermosa Beach, California

125

This page, upper right:
175. Forrest Myers. *250 Miles Per Hour.* Chaise lounge. 1980.
Aluminum, imron paint, 32 × 84 × 36".
Art et Industrie, New York

This page, lower right:
176. Forrest Myers. *Fold Chair.*
Side chair. 1971.
Anodized aluminum, 35 × 17 × 17".
Art et Industrie, New York

Opposite, above:
177. Forrest Myers. *Stand-Up Table.* 1982.
Anodized aluminum and glass, height: 40";
diameter: 46" (overall).
Courtesy Furniture of the Twentieth Century,
New York

Opposite, below:
178. Forrest Myers. *Cut Out.* Easy chair. 1971.
Anodized aluminum, 33 × 25 × 42".
Art et Industrie, New York

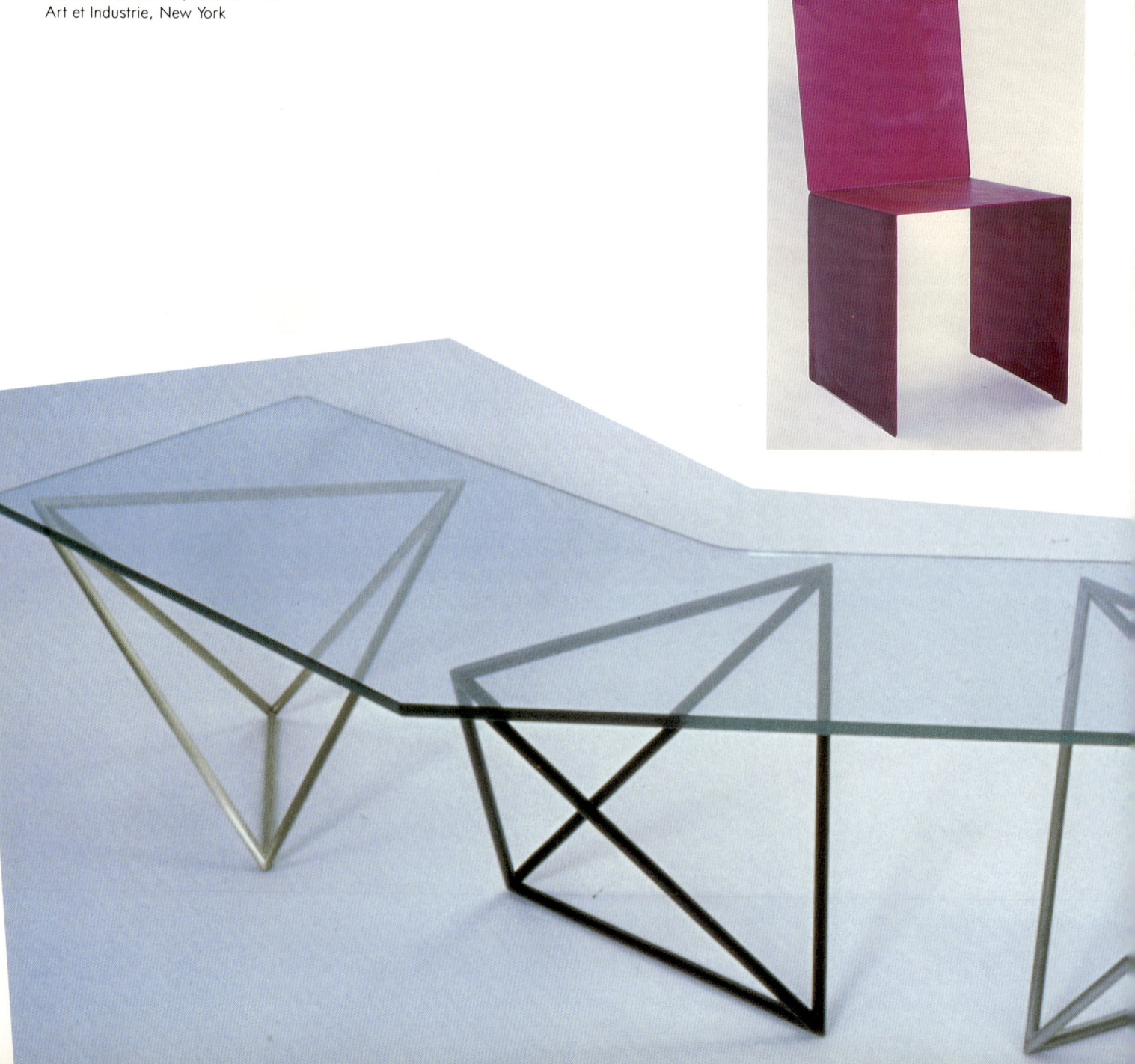

Forrest Myers

Born in Long Beach, California, 1941
Lives in New York

I've been thinking about furniture design for as long as I've been an artist. Having dealt with the aesthetic and technical problems of sculpture, the application of those principles to furniture was a natural transition. I'm still dealing with the question of which is conceptually most important, my art or my furniture, but I find the discovery of a creative idea holds the same excitement.

I started by designing two chairs in 1971: the *Fold Chair*, cut and folded from a single sheet of aluminum so it could be anodized a bright color—a form-follows-function idea—and the *Cut-Out* easy chair, bent in three sections so it too could be anodized and screwed together. Then on the basis of the few designs I had, I was offered a one-man show in New York in 1980. As I set about building the furniture for the show, I realized that the strongest aspect of my ideas lay in the structure itself. I wanted to reinvent the basic support systems for tables, chairs, and so on. The only decoration I allowed myself was the inherent color of the materials: steel, brass, stainless steel, and the anodized colors that fuse to the surface of aluminum. I had been exploring the colors of these metals for quite some time in my sculpture. Having studied Buckminster Fuller's work on structural polyhedra, particularly tetrahedrons, the idea of getting the tetrahedron to do something new seemed unlikely. The exciting moment came with the discovery that three tetrahedrons on their sides, a configuration that ordinarily would collapse, become a rigid support system when topped with glass. The flat plane of the glass rights the tetrahedron and becomes an integral part of the support structure itself. The heavier the glass, the more solid the table becomes, unlike a conventional one. The illusion that the tetrahedrons are balancing on their own defies our conception of gravity.

[Continued]

179. Forrest Myers. Geodyssey. Coffee table. 1980.
Brass, steel, stainless steel, 14 × 60 × 29″.
Art et Industrie, New York

The *Park Place* coffee table, part of a series of tables designed for small apartments, is a tension/compression structure. The two tetrahedrons are welded inside one another without touching. They are held apart by a single stainless steel wire that connects the two at opposite points. The six remaining wires bring the structure into compression so it becomes rigid. The visual tension and the formidable strength-to-weight ratio become a main part of its aesthetic.

The *250 Miles Per Hour* chaise lounge may well read as an abstract sculpture before one realizes it functions.

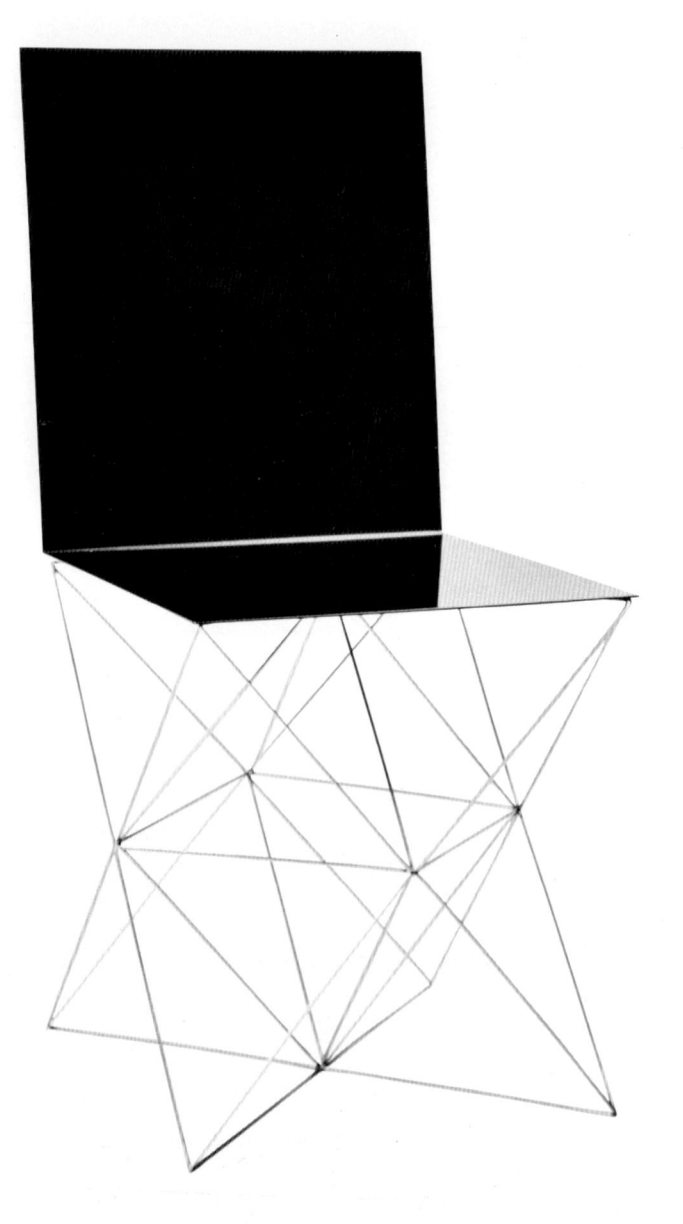

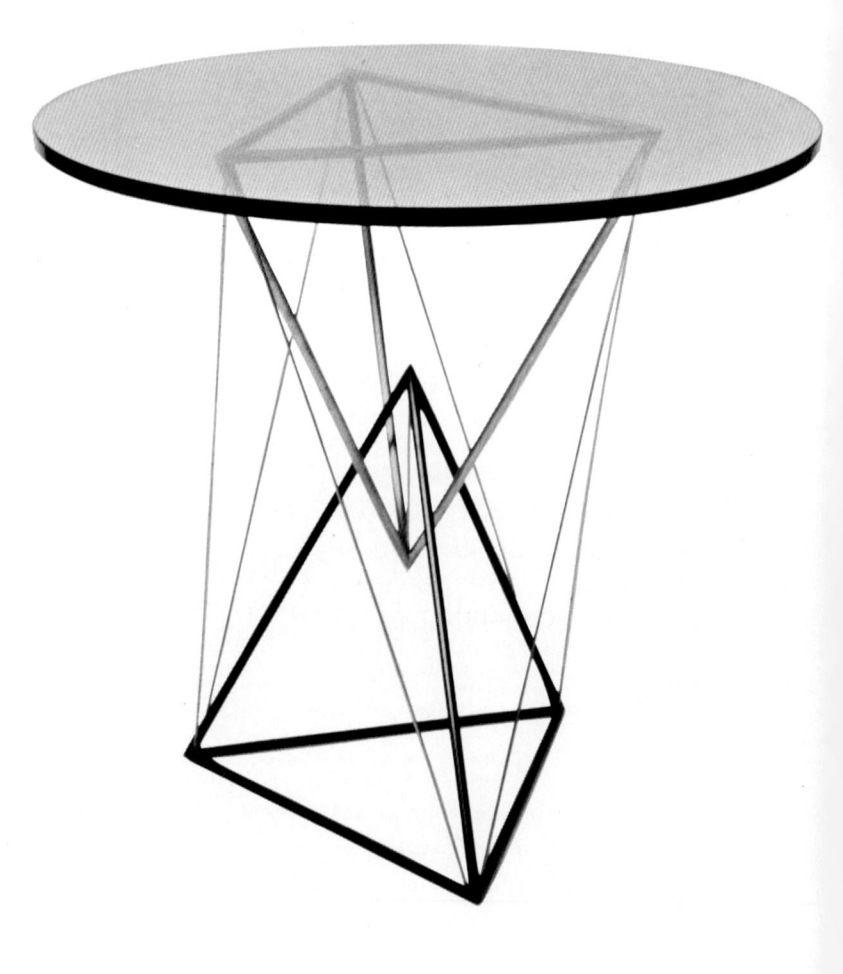

181. Forrest Myers. *Park Place*. Cafe table. 1980. Steel, stainless steel, 30×20×20″.
Art et Industrie, New York

180. Forrest Myers. *Wedding Gift*. Side chair. 1980. Painted stainless steel, 35×17×17″.
Art et Industrie, New York

Richard Nonas

Born in Brooklyn, New York, 1936
Lives in New York

In all the work I do I'm interested in making objects of which every part is clear and makes perfect sense, but in which the end result is somehow more than it should be, given the simplicity of the elements. I build the chairs the same way I build my sculpture; that is, in the most direct way and in the way that has the most to do with accentuating the properties that interest me in the material. In the case of the chairs, it was the rough, heavy wood with its strength and its ability to support itself over very long spans. The material came out of the false floor of my loft, which gave me an endless supply of four-by-eights from which I built the whole place, including the furniture.

Since I like to lean back on a chair and I was using the heavy wood, I made the seat longer to create a counterweight when one leans back. The balance is different than one would expect, and an unconscious move becomes a conscious one, which is interesting to me. The chairs have an amusing, almost cartoonlike quality, and I like the way they feel as well as how they look.

After I made the chairs I saw there was very little difference between them and my sculpture in the way they felt, in the way they were put together, in the kind of objects they seemed to be. But as I thought about it, the difference became apparent: no matter how much they looked like the sculpture, no matter how strong, simple, and direct they were, they were still chairs. An abstract sculpture doesn't have that set of connotations, that sense of being one member of a large class of objects primarily defined by use.

The chairs are very definitely furniture and very definitely sculpture as well. A lot of the small wooden sculptural pieces that I make function as stools or as tables, but they also have an existence without an identity as furniture. They are only recognized as furniture when they are used that way.

182. Richard Nonas.
Two Chairs. 1982.
Pine, 46½ × 9½ × 24".
Courtesy Oil & Steel Gallery, New York

Masayuki Oda

Born in Tokyo, Japan, 1950
Lives in Los Angeles

There are innumerable materials a sculptor can choose from. As the range of these materials expands, the more crucial it becomes to grasp each one's characteristics: its hardness, its softness, its particular subtle color, its tactile or dynamic quality, and so on. I make sculpture by putting elements together from my own criterion in the simplest way. Through minimized process and simplicity, I want the piece to achieve maximum conceptual expression.

Some of my pieces are placed low to the ground, others are higher—table or bench height. The objects become functional; people can get involved physically with them by sitting on them or by placing things on them. It is amusing to think that my work can inhabit a space not only as a piece of sculpture but also as something else.

Robert Rauschenberg

Born in Port Arthur, Texas, 1925
Lives in Captiva Island, Florida, and New York

As a rule I hate furniture. I have as little of it as possible. My aesthetics are still a little loft-bound. I prefer big, open, clear spaces. I like to see at least three corners of a room at once, so I have a tendency to put everything in one place and that sharpens up the rest of the room.

I hadn't thought of making furniture until I was asked to do so on a whim at an afternoon buffet at Leo Castelli's gallery. I made the prototypes and the pieces were made up by a cabinetmaker.

I like the *Cardboard Table* because it looks even more useless in a photograph than it does in real life. The tables contained in it are collapsible and rearrangeable; there are all kinds of hinges and ways to turn them around and make them half the size. Parts of the table are at seating level. You can jump on it too because it has all been reinforced. There is a cardboard outer shell that has been treated for permanence and water resistance. I think of it as an eccentric folding table and chairs.

The *Water Table* has focused lights passing through a tub of water mounted in a rectangle and enclosed in sandblasted plastic. When you move the can around, the whole table becomes a seascape that I projected onto the surface. I think everybody was worried about it springing a leak, particularly because it was made by an artist like me. I don't think I contributed any confidence to the project; everyone knows what a great craftsman I am.

I work with chairs and lights, and tires and lights, and all those things because I like objects that cast their own shadows. The *Tire Lamp* was just another item that related to that idea.

184. Robert Rauschenberg.
Tire Lamp. 1971.
Tire, incandescent lamp,
diameter: 26".
Collection the artist, New York

183. Masayuki Oda.
Bench. 1982.
Concrete, wood, paint,
16 × 22 × 14".
Collection the artist,
Los Angeles

185. Robert Rauschenberg. *Cardboard Table*. 1971.
Wood, rope, cardboard, hardware, 24 × 96 × 36".
Fabricator: Styria Studio, New York,
for Daedalus Concepts.
Private collection, New York

186. Robert Rauschenberg. *Water Table.* 1971.
Sandblasted glass, Plexiglas, water,
paint can, wood, metal,
electrical fixtures, 24 × 48 × 24".
Courtesy Leo Castelli Gallery, New York

134

Roland Reiss

Born in Chicago, 1929
Lives in Venice, California

I make small-scale environments, and the objects within these "miniature narrative tableaux" operate as signifiers, so they are generalized but clear. The mind's associations guide you through the scenarios.

Most of my work deals with social or philosophic themes. I use the language of cultural styles to make statements out of the relationships between objects. The choice of an individual object has its own stylistic cut and meaning, and when it is put in combination with other forms, that meaning builds on a number of levels.

Spaces are expressive, and we express ourselves in those spaces; the objects that inhabit them, the styles, the way space is handled all govern that to some degree. It's tied up with furniture and architecture. I got interested in didactically illustrating that kind of experience on a life-size scale. Two interconnected layers interested me: one was proxemics, the investigation of cultural space, the ways we distance ourselves and so on, and the other was body language. I found that physical engagement became a critical tool for getting the kinds of experiences I wanted, and that led me to the concept of the steel piece in which I could confront functionality, explore body position and attitude, the nature of materials, and the structure and distribution of objects in space. I saw the steel chair as a prototype for a life-size tableau largely based on muscle-builders' furniture, still generalized but part fiction, with that kind of static placement and operative space around each piece. I wanted to press the physical nature of furniture design and set up a series of planes that would dump your body in difficult positions. In this piece the angle of vision is set up at forty-five degrees. As an isolated piece, the design of the steel chair was really meant to develop the sense of your own physical weight and its position in space.

187. Roland Reiss. *Body Language I.*
Chair. 1980.
Steel, 48 × 60 × 18".
Flow Ace Gallery, Venice, California

GOOD BYE

Leo Sewell

Born in Annapolis, Maryland, 1945
Lives in Philadelphia

For the last ten years I've been a high-culture hermit, steeping myself deeply in my trash and TV. I pick up trash nearly every morning and use it for fuel, clothes, furnishings, amusement, and assemblages. My work is entirely made up of what Philadelphia throws away, assembled into shapes that give me pleasure. To directly recycle is satisfying for me.

I grew up near a dump. My father had a shop and taught me how to assemble the industrial discards I treasured. I had little awareness of what art was or its relevance to my work until I met art history. I went to the University of Delaware and in reaction to the lack of imagination and humor I found there, I made eighteenth-century furniture pieces out of twentieth-century junk. I realized that I had to keep academic inquiry from interfering with whatever individual statement I had to make. I traded in my *Art in America* for *Scientific American* and my Museum of Modern Art membership for Roller Derby tickets.

As a sculptor I have always described my aesthetic as "horror vacui." The same with the furniture. In fact I make no real distinction between my sculpture and my furniture.

188. Leo Sewell. *Mantle Clock*. 1981.
Reclaimed objects, 22 × 14 × 5".
Collection the artist, Philadelphia

189. Leo Sewell. *Grandmother Clock*. 1981.
Reclaimed objects, 70 × 14 × 8".
Collection the artist, Philadelphia

190. Leo Sewell. *Table*. 1981.
Reclaimed objects, 25 × 22 × 19".
Collection the artist, Philadelphia

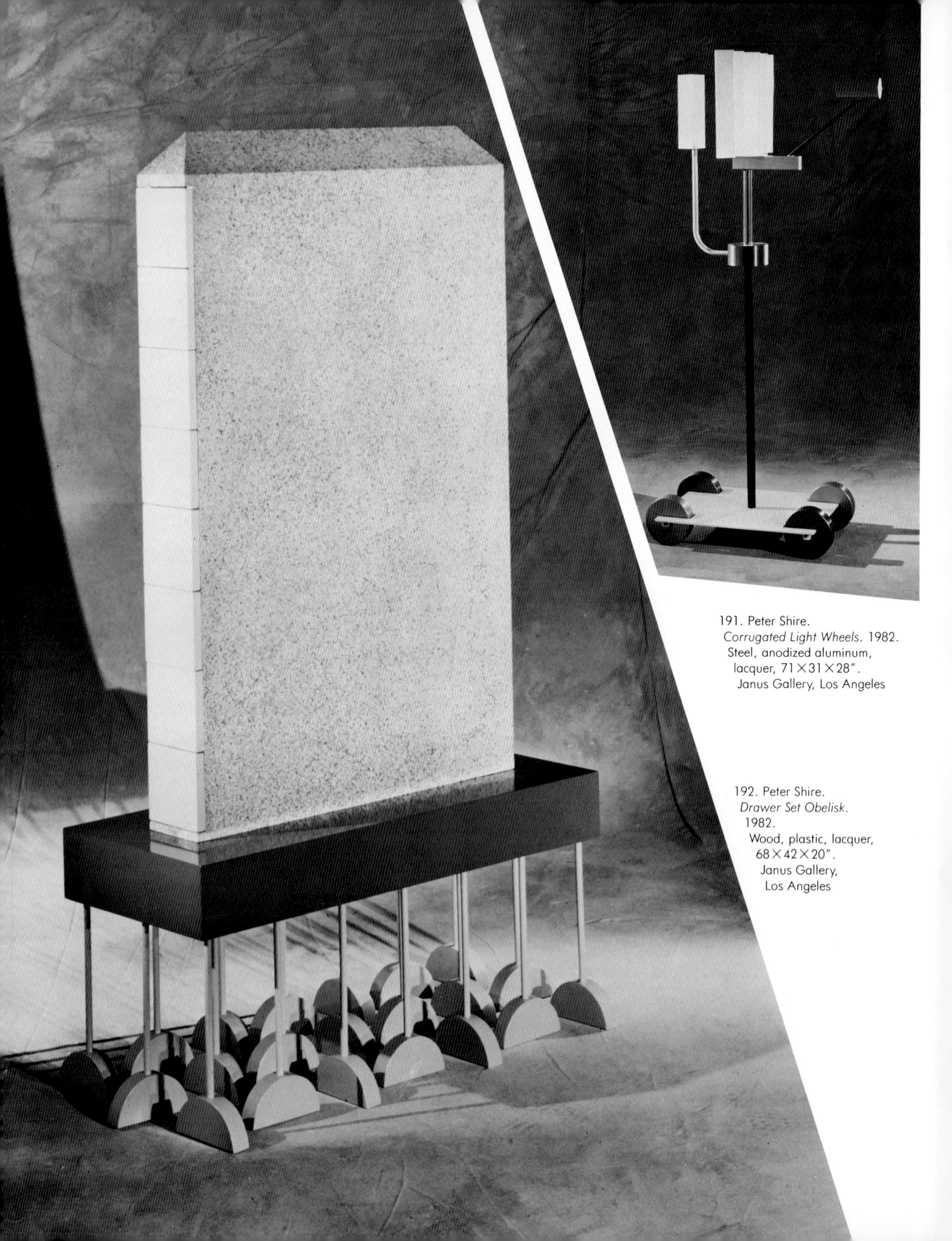

191. Peter Shire.
Corrugated Light Wheels. 1982.
Steel, anodized aluminum,
lacquer, 71×31×28".
Janus Gallery, Los Angeles

192. Peter Shire.
Drawer Set Obelisk.
1982.
Wood, plastic, lacquer,
68×42×20".
Janus Gallery,
Los Angeles

193. Peter Shire.
Henry (Freestanding Shelf). 1982.
Wood, steel, lacquer, 47×39×18".
Collection Jacob and Ruth Bloom, Los Angeles

Peter Shire

Born in Los Angeles, 1947
Lives in Los Angeles

As a Californian I tend to be influenced by abstract formalism, asymmetrical architectonics, and the warm colors of Mexico. My background is in ceramics, so function has always been a starting point for me. However crazy and fanciful my work appears, I'm still held by function. The teapots I make are borderline, however. They're more involved with a group of shapes and a material; I know how to push that material, and its limits keep moving farther and farther out. Making furniture has given me a chance to break my scale barriers with ceramics without being hampered by the materials. Every material has its limitations and suggests and calls for different applications.

In all the work I do I prefer the simple, direct approach. Like my teapots, my furniture deals more with combinations of shapes and volumes. I'm after the direct relationship of two forms interacting without extra fussiness. What it's all about for me is visually imagining something and giving life to it in its concrete form. I don't like it when a piece is so finished and precious that the fun is gone. I want to create a unique situation where there is mystery and a theatricality that people can respond to and interact with. I want people to live with my pieces and have a little magic world.

194. Peter Shire. *Secret Springs*. 1982.
Steel, anodized aluminum, glass, lacquer,
29½×48×48".
Collection Larry and Inge Horner, Los Angeles

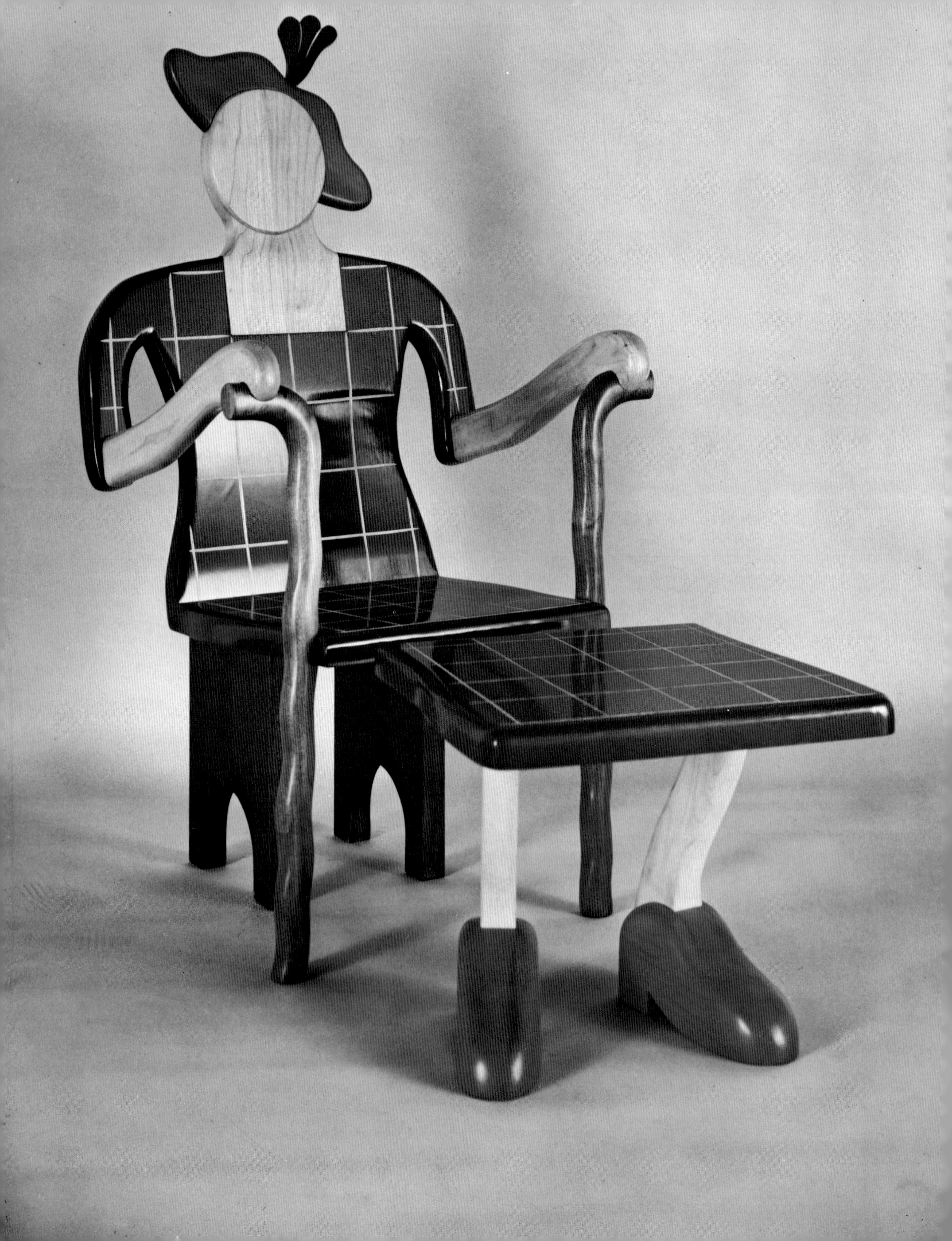

Left:
195. Alan Siegel. *Big Julie*. 1982.
Poplar, black walnut, paint,
51 × 28 × 45".
Courtesy Nancy Hoffman
Gallery, New York

Alan Siegel

Born in New York, 1938
Lives in New York

I've always been a painter, but in the sixties I wanted to shape more than what the painting surface allowed me, and so I began putting things on the canvas that started to come off the wall onto the floor. Then about 1964 I was living near the beach and big pieces of wood constantly washed up; it seemed crazy not to use them. I decided to make a chair and found it a terrific relief to do something that disappeared when somebody sat on it and didn't take the space of art.

Over the years one of the greatest pleasures in making the chairs has been to saturate a three-dimensional object with color. I don't consider the chairs any less or any more than the other things I paint. I'm just lucky enough to make what I find myself compelled to make whether it is a chair, another construction, or something that hangs on the wall.

A chair is so directional in its attitude in space that just to take that skeleton, that structure, and put it in space is to make a very convincing three-dimensional form. Chairs mimic human form and scale, and for better or worse I have a strong anthropomorphic tendency. Many of my chairs are literally figures; others are creatures, most recently, sea creatures. I usually make a "family" of chairs because they tend to develop in an associational way with one another.

When I make a chair I feel freed of the obligations to what I've been taught about high art, so more of my humor is likely to materialize. My main influences in making the chairs are American folk art and African art. I like the way the carving is filled with humorous invention. It always seems a happier expression when something can be said with wit instead of solemnity.

Above:
196. Alan Siegel. *Star Fish*. 1981.
Poplar, stain, 42½ × 41 × 21".
Courtesy Nancy Hoffman Gallery, New York

197. Alan Siegel.
Shell.
1982.
Hardwood, paint,
41 × 30 × 24".
Courtesy Nancy Hoffman Gallery,
New York

198. Alan Siegel.
Momma with Twins. 1982.
Painted and stained poplar,
45 × 63 × 22".
Courtesy Nancy Hoffman Gallery,
New York

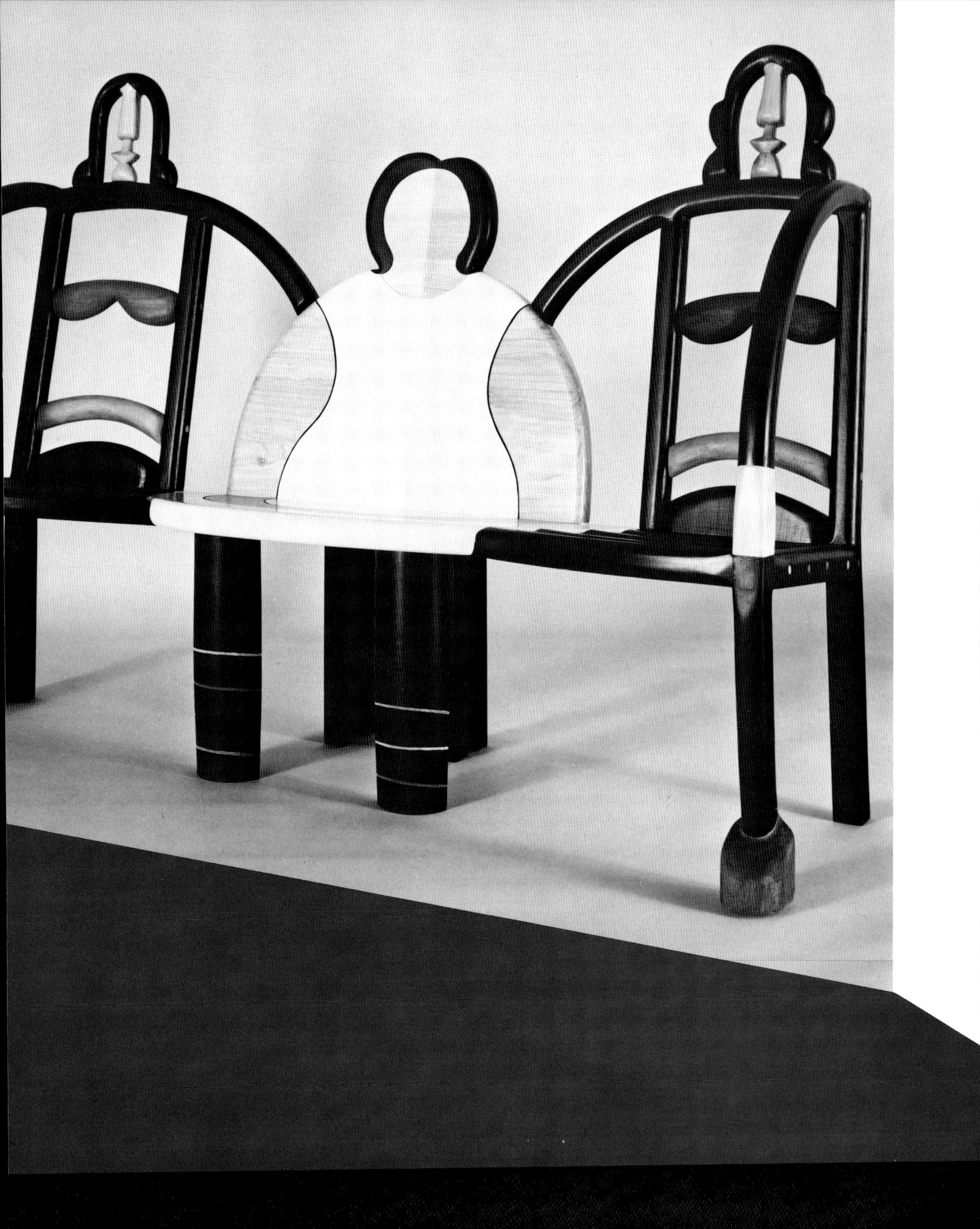

199. Buster Simpson and Randy Turner. *Living Bench*. 1980. One-half-inch clear Plexiglas, tubular metal, concrete, eight living indigenous willow trees. Courtesy Duvall Public Library, City of Duvall, Washington, and King County Arts Commission, Washington. Photo taken in 1981

Buster Simpson

Born in Saginaw, Michigan, 1942
Lives in Seattle, Washington

I designed the *Living Bench* project with Randy Turner, a bent-willow furniture maker who lives in Duvall, Washington. For the piece we used clear Plexiglas molded into a bench shape, supported with a tubular metal frame, and secured with concrete footing, along with a row of eight one-year-old willow root balls that were cut off the first year and sprouted. The fact that the bench is clear allows the willows to hug the interior of the Plexiglas form as they grow. If the bench had been opaque, the saplings would have tried to avoid it in the growing process. Over the years the willows will grow up the back of the bench to a height of seven or eight feet, and each of the shoots will be manipulated to form a kind of woven crown canopy. In five years or so the Plexiglas mold will be pulled off, and people will be able to sit directly on the tree.

We chose a Metro bus stop in front of the Duvall Public Library for the site, and on the bench is a note inviting people to go into the library, where a scrapbook about the project is on file.

My work is about transformation and accentuation of the environment. What I like to do is take the mundaneness of a situation and capitalize on it to achieve what is right for the space. As an idealist and pragmatist, I'm interested in getting the work out there in the public context.

Miriam Slater

Born in Inglewood, California, 1952
Lives in Los Angeles

I started taking faux-finish courses (a finish used in trompe l'oeil) because I wanted to learn more old-master painting techniques and that was the only course available to me at the time. Once I learned it, it became lucrative to do furniture, and I got very involved in it. I've put faux-finishes on floors, walls, phones, furniture, fireplaces, everything.

In my work I'm aiming toward meshing the great European traditions of France and Italy with something I can say. I want to blow on the paint and say it all with a few brushstrokes, but I know it will take a long time to develop that depth and richness. In the meantime I dip into various styles and periods and try them out for a while to see where I stand. Whatever period I jump into invariably results in a piece of furniture. Previously I overlapped and wrapped the images around the given object or piece of furniture. The *Cubist Table* is really the first time I have worked from scratch in three dimensions. Cubism symbolizes getting back to the basics: the straight line, the curve, and structure.

I'll always do furniture. It offers me a different perspective and freedom from the serious formality of the rectangle.

200. Miriam Slater.
Cubist Table. 1983.
Oil paint, wood,
22 × 16 × 12".
Collection Mr. Jack Nicholson,
Los Angeles

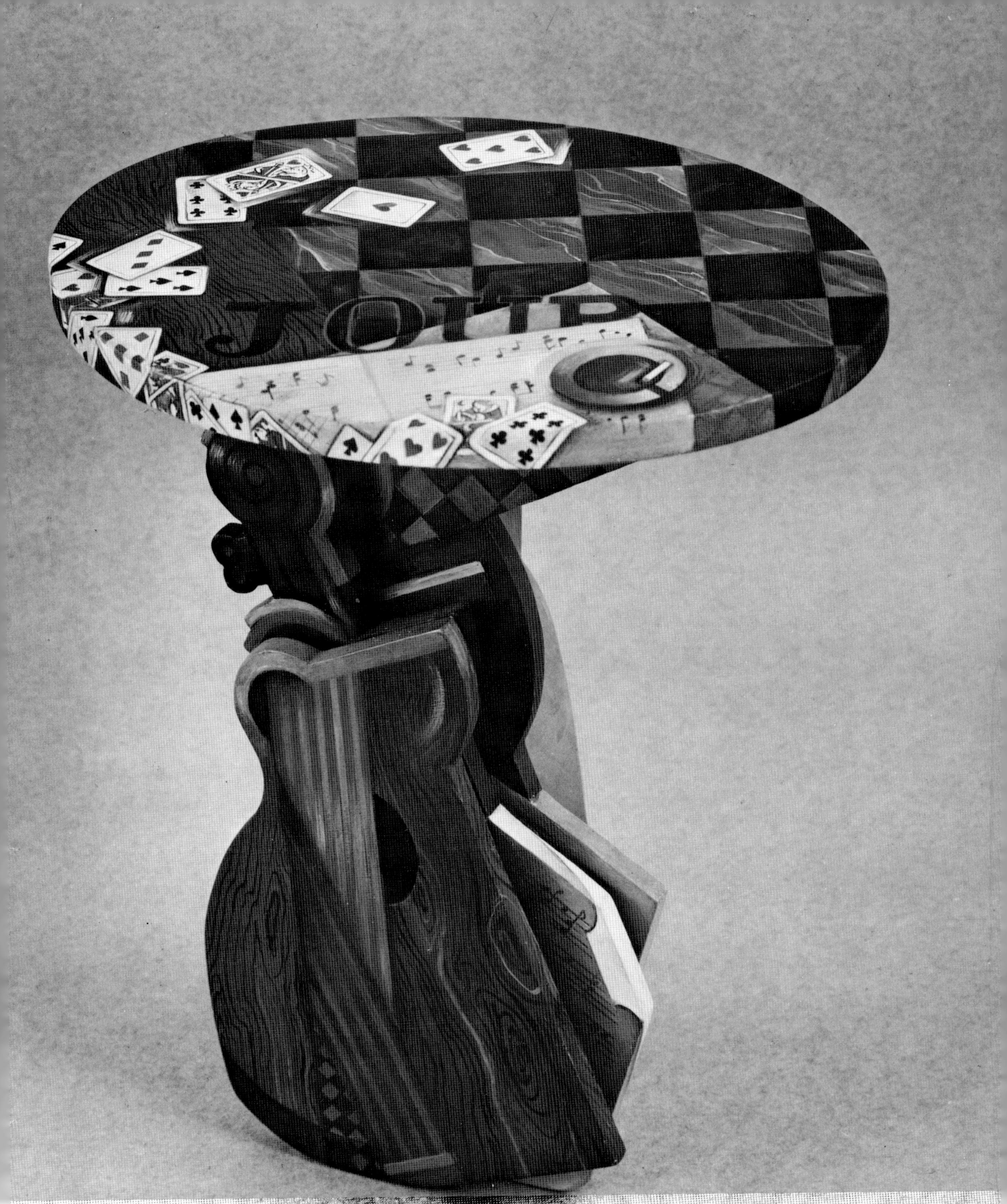

201. Carmen Spera. *Urban Cactus*. Vanity. 1982. Wood, glass, paint, mirror, 30×60×24". Art et Industrie, New York

202. Carmen Spera. *Crosshatch*. Table. 1982. Glass, paint, 18×42×30". Art et Industrie, New York

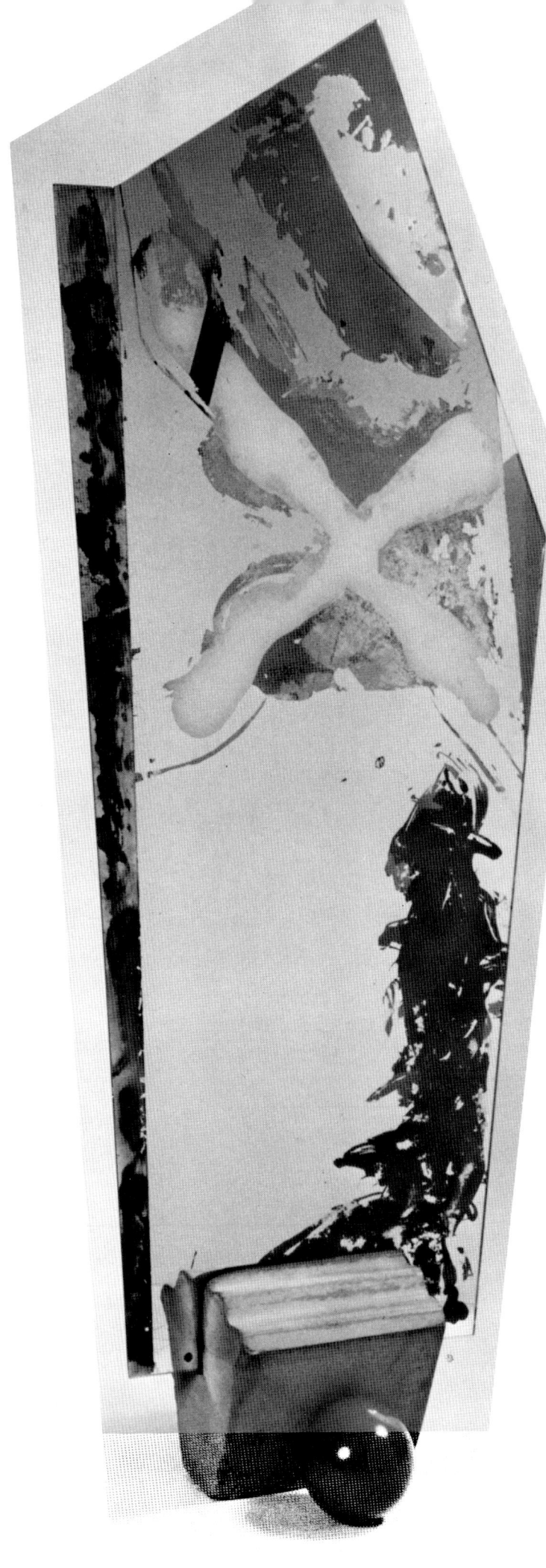

Carmen Spera

Born in New York, 1951
Lives in New York

I've always drawn and done collages, constructions, and small dioramas. I grew up on TV, so I'm used to seeing things framed in boxes. In the little dioramas I made paper furniture that was out of kilter. These pieces were my first models, and I thought it would be nice to build them as life-size props. One day while doing the constructions I ran out of paper, so I started playing with a piece of glass I had around. The minute I touched it I fell in love with the idea of painting on it.

After doing several of these paintings, I thought of making a tabletop. I referred back to the original dioramas and began to think of the glass as paper, cutting it, fitting it, and gluing it in the same way. I liked using all glass with no hardware. Functionality then became another boundary to work with, and taking the piece as far out sculpturally as I could gave it that much more of an edge.

The exciting part of glass is that it's like dealing with fire. Though it is solid, I try to get the work to look dangerous, as though it could collapse and shatter into a million pieces.

I think art or furniture should reflect the age it's in. There are certain materials that resonate with the times, like bronze or marble did at one point. To me this is the glass age because it expresses the idea of accident and the fragility of the situation where the end of the world is a real possibility. But rather than give in to despair, my pieces are festive, a celebration of the apocalypse, the exciting, frightening tension that is ours to work with.

203. Carmen Spera. *Zabella's Big Mirror*. 1982.
Mirror, paint, cement, wood, 84×30".
Art et Industrie, New York

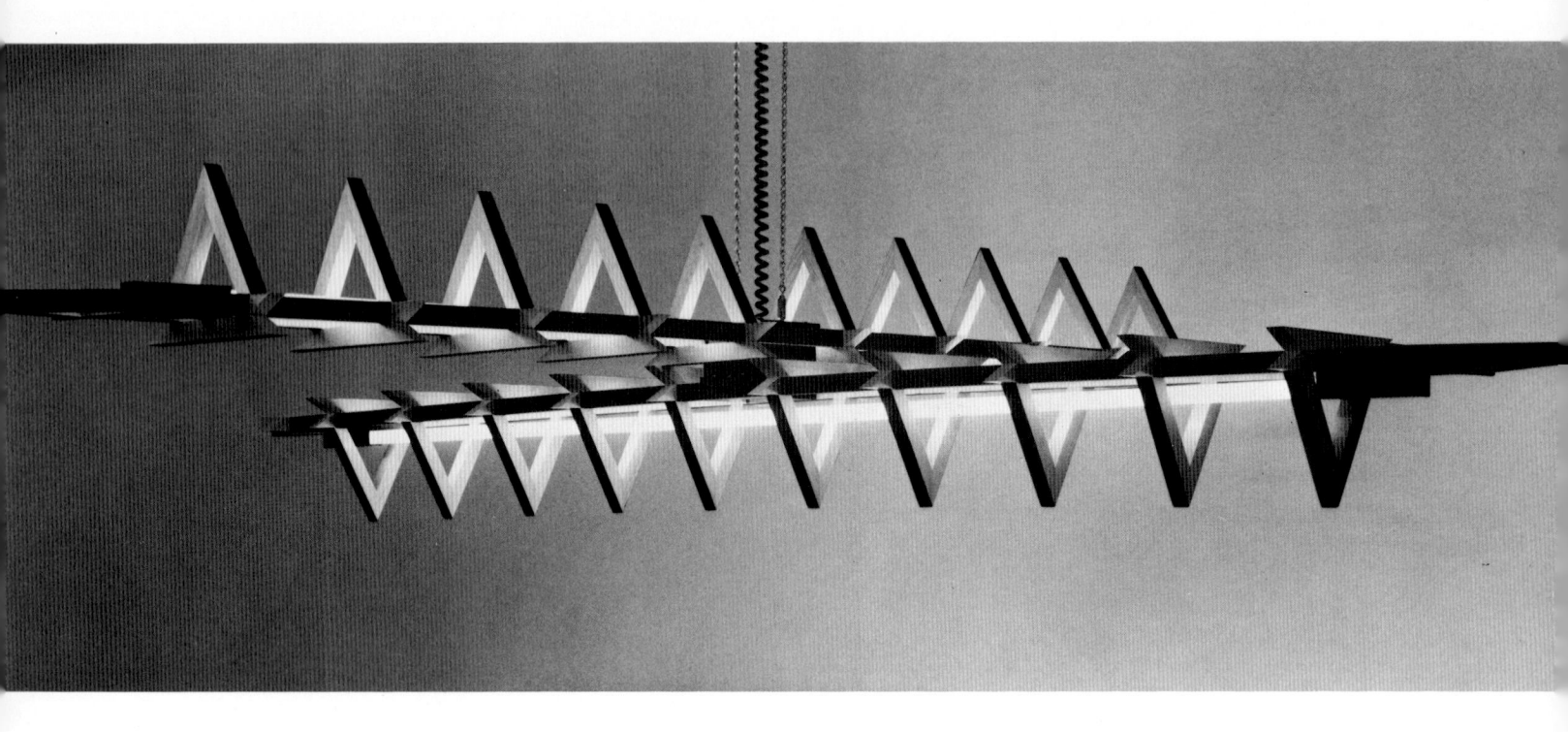

204. Christopher Sproat.
Adirondack Chandelier. 1981.
Pine, paint, plastic, neon, 9'8" × 9'8" × 18". Courtesy the artist, New York

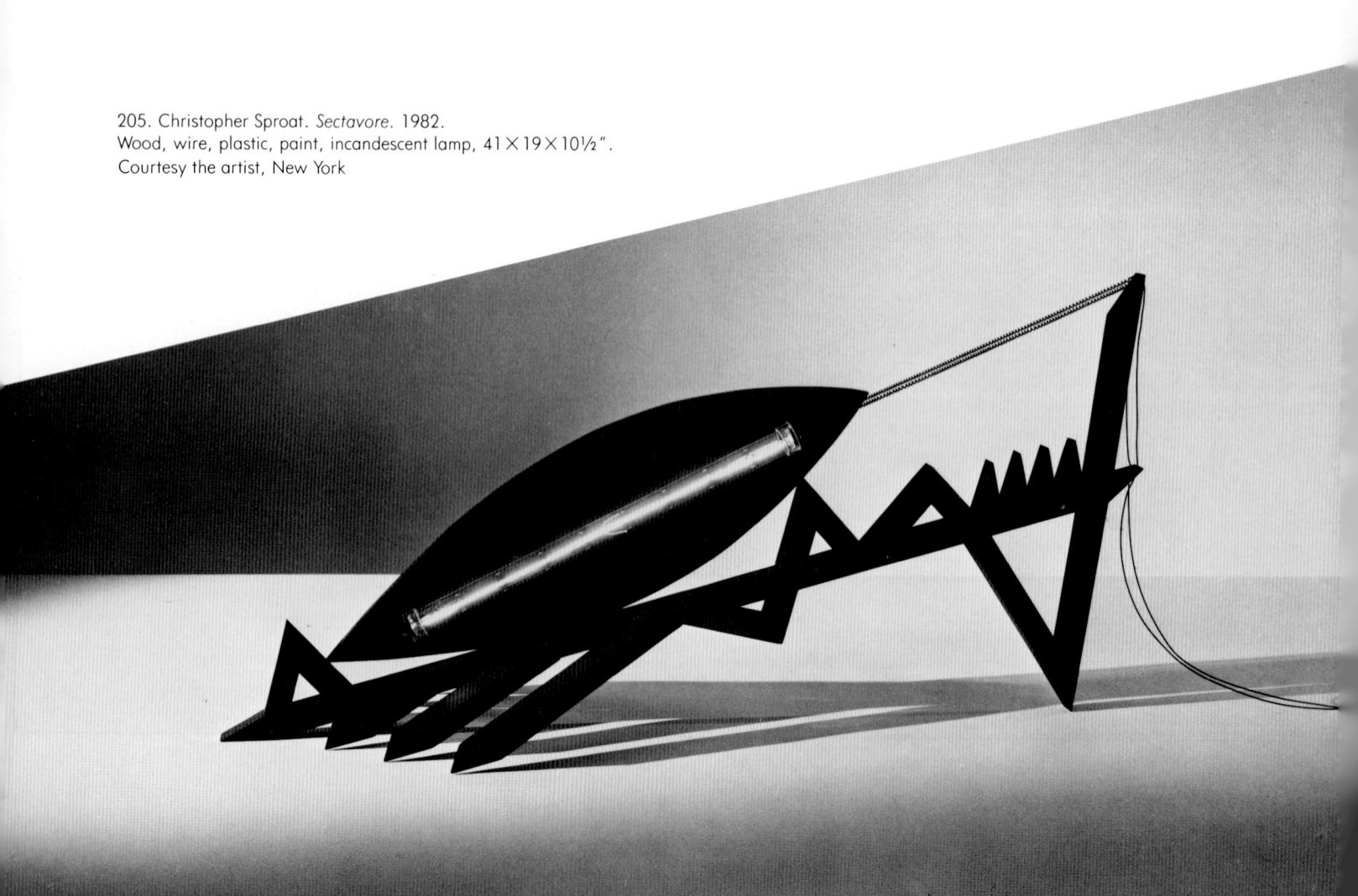

205. Christopher Sproat. *Sectavore.* 1982.
Wood, wire, plastic, paint, incandescent lamp, 41 × 19 × 10½".
Courtesy the artist, New York

Christopher Sproat

Born in Boston, Massachusetts, 1945
Lives in New York

In 1975 a fire destroyed everything I had, including my art, and I had to make all my furniture over again. My father died shortly after the fire, and the first things I made were three chairs. I realized I was making a family portrait, and that excited me because it meant I could put the making of furniture into a more metaphorical realm. Besides satisfying the practical requirements, I could make references to the rest of the world.

I see this as being a very stark age, so my color limitation fits the statements I'm trying to convey. Black is the way life feels to me. I don't see it as depressing; to me it is sexual, sensual, ultramale, and ultrafemale. I'm kind of a puritan, and I like the starkness of black and white. What color there is has been the natural color of the wood and the blue, white, lavender, and red of the gases in the neon tubes.

There are all kinds of traces in my work that have to do with death, presence, and absence. Bones, skeletons, and hand prints are among the kinds of traces that I use. In a way a chair is a trace of a human presence. It is an empty receptacle in which you put the associations you want. I also make references to other forms of life, which furniture usually doesn't concern itself with.

There is a lot of gesture in what I do whether it is vertical gesture or slight angles that go back and forth from a central core. I see a lot of relationship between my furniture and the design of insect bodies. The angles are similar, and I try to make them thin and delicate with the visual strength and muscularity of a spider or black ant.

Above:
206. Christopher Sproat.
Leaf Back. 1981.
Edition of 6.
Wood, satin, enamel,
44 × 22 × 32".
Courtesy the artist, New York

207. George Sugarman. *Dining Table*. 1982. Aluminum, paint, 29 × 144 × 48". Collection Mr. and Mrs. Asher Edelman, New York

George Sugarman

Born in New York, 1912
Lives in New York

I do a lot of public sculpture. In thinking about it and what it does and why we put it there, I realized there was a whole dimension to art other than the precious, elite attitude of museums and galleries. In a piece of public sculpture, people are actually invited to walk in, sit on it, climb on it, and that brings up the idea of art as a participatory thing. Bringing the dimension of use into my art does not lower my own aesthetic standards. A work of art has a purpose, and different purposes elicit different works of art. I don't believe art can be abstracted from the world; we're social beings, and art is a social statement.

The imagery of the *Multiple Approach* was very much a continuity of the relief collages I had been doing; I didn't use a particular imagery specifically for them. The images are abstract, and like all abstract things, you can see anything you want in them. I thought of the screen as a work of art that could be placed in a room as a divider.

The *Dining Table* was a commission. If it had simply been one of my low sculptures, I would not have made the flat top. Actually it worked out beautifully because the glass establishes the plane and you can look inside which is even more exciting and dramatic. I had to think about people sitting around it so the support has continuous accordionlike angles against which I played the more organic forms. I got a chair and tested all the angles and they worked out fine. Doing the table was a pleasurable experience. I like dealing with practical problems because it broadens you and makes you do things differently.

208. George Sugarman. *Multiple Approach*. 1978.
Wood, acrylic-painted paper,
foam-core board, fiberglass, epoxy, 81×81".
Robert Miller Gallery, New York

209. Paula Sweet. *Table with Water and Fish*. 1981.
Glass, plastic, steel, height: 34"; diameter: 48".
Courtesy L. A. Louver Gallery, Venice, California

210. Paula Sweet. *Tiffany Light*. 1981.
Wire, paper, photographic slides, height: 16"; diameter: 36".
Courtesy L. A. Louver Gallery, Venice, California

Paula Sweet

Born in Berwyn, Illinois, 1949
Lives in New York

I make rugs and lights and tables and drawings and ceramic dishes and paintings and dresses, and each thing I make has a purpose, even if it is a single mark on a piece of paper.

Everything in my house has to be movable and functional, and because my things evolve out of a particular personal need and oftentimes must serve multipurposes in a small space, I end up making them myself. It is never a concern of mine whether or not these objects are art. A dish is a dish, a dress is a dress, a painting is a painting.

My lights evolved out of a desire for a certain soft light and color in the room. I chose to make them out of paper because of its light weight, transparency, and ease of folding for storage. I like working with paper because I can cut out shapes that make colors and shadows on the walls. I can adapt the size and shape to fit any space. Some stand on the ground and some hang from the ceiling.

When I moved to Manhattan I missed my Los Angeles garden and fish ponds. In my loft I needed a desk, a dining table, and a garden, and it occurred to me that I could combine all three. I had already made a water table out of wood in Los Angeles. It had no glass on top and you could set your plate on stepping stones and eat right on the water, enjoying the sounds and the reflections of my lights in it. This table is a more practical application of the same feeling. My garden is in constant change: sometimes it has goldfish or turtles in it, or newts and green grass, and sometimes it is a desert with cacti.

211. Paula Sweet. *Light Tower*. 1982.
Paper with reinforced steel,
height: 96"; diameter: 42".
Courtesy L. A. Louver Gallery,
Venice, California

Below, left:
212. Michael Todd. *White Water Lily Table I*. 1980–82.
Bronze-plated steel, paint, 22½ × 34 × 34".
Courtesy the artist, Los Angeles

Michael Todd

Born in Omaha, Nebraska, 1935
Lives in Los Angeles

213. Michael Todd.
Kandinsky Table. 1980.
Lacquered steel,
21¾ × 51½ × 36".
Courtesy the artist, Los Angeles

I made my first sculpture-table in 1969. It was really a sculpture that incidentally could function as a table. The second and third pieces were made for my home and garden, and since then I've made many for friends with the thought that they could function as tables. The tables became a way to surprise myself and to flirt with the idea of function in relation to form.

The sculpture-tables are not as ambitious as the "pure" sculpture, but occasionally one emerges that seems more profound. The tables have many elements in common with my other sculpture, and once I brought the concept of "table" into the sculpture per se, my work became more metaphorical, eccentric, and free-form.

I tend to see sculpture as an intellectual, emotional, and spiritual endeavor. I feed off painting and Oriental calligraphy a great deal, and I see the sculpture-tables in painterly terms. They have splashes of steel, rather than splashes of color, and rings, lines, and planes that are "drawn" or "painted" out in space. There is also something about their lowness to the ground that tends to make them read like paintings in depth. I equate a tabletop with an elevated ground plane or water level, and perhaps that parallelism is the formal problem that keeps the idea of the table alive for me. I've always loved the Bauhaus attitude toward furniture as art, and I share the Eastern sentiment that a raku teacup can be a great aesthetic experience. I'm totally against the idea that when something has a function it is not art, so it was easy for me to attempt some tables of my own. I seem to take them more and more seriously as time passes, and I keep doing them.

214. Michael Todd. *Homage to Claude Monet*. 1969.
Painted steel, 18 × 96 × 54".
Courtesy the artist, Los Angeles

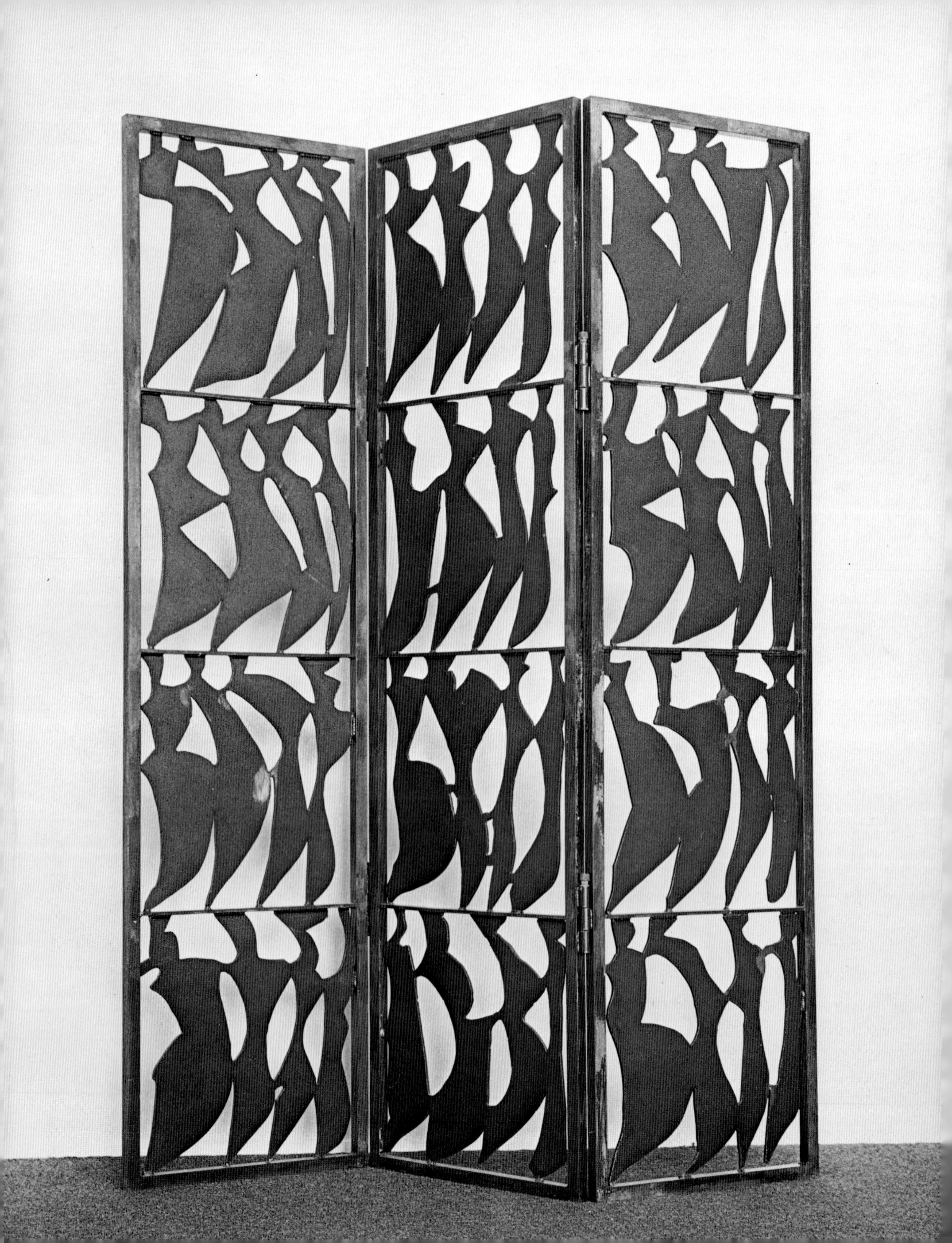

Opposite:
215. Ernest Trova. *Screen.* 1977.
Painted steel, 72 × 45".
Collection the artist,
St. Louis, Missouri

Ernest Trova

Born in St. Louis, Missouri, 1927
Lives in St. Louis

My work is a process in which one thing leads to another. I work very much in series and make many variations based on the motifs in my drawings and paintings. In 1947 I began professionally, doing Expressionistic figurative works. In the late fifties I developed the image of the "falling man," which was a simplified version of a silhouette of a figure. I also did environmental things where the whole room was part of the art piece and the paintings were actually assemblage works. My work during the sixties included two- and three-dimensional assemblages and freestanding constructions. My recent "poet series," which I've been working on since 1980, is an echo of the earliest Expressionistic painting. So within each series my art has taken many forms and variations.

Because the screens are based on calligraphic drawings, they contain a see-through element. This is consistent with the original paintings, so that the screens are again a variation of the calligraphic motif with some liberties thrown in. In answer to the question "Are they art?" I believe they are. They are sculpture that can be used to divide a room. The tables are pieces of sculpture that become functional objects because of the use of legs and a glass top. The panel that is the tabletop could just as well be hung on the wall as a plaque. For me the idea of making furniture is very much a side issue.

216. Ernest Trova. *Untitled Table.* 1977.
Painted steel, height: 14½"; diameter: 24".
Hokin Gallery, Inc., Palm Beach, Florida

217. Alwy Visschedyk.
Knock-Down Lounge Chair. 1978.
Birch plywood, 28 × 30 × 30".
Collection Denise Domergue,
Los Angeles

218. Alwy Visschedyk.
Knock-Down Chair. 1978.
Birch plywood,
33 × 18 × 23½".
Collection the artist,
Los Angeles

Alwy Visschedyk

Born in Maasbracht, Holland, 1946
Lives in Los Angeles

I started making chairs at sixteen while growing up in Australia. I began to make furniture again in 1976 because I had a lot of ideas for it and I liked making it. I respect Mies van der Rohe and Le Corbusier as furniture designers; they took their materials as far as they could. My work is very different from theirs, and that has to do with time and place, but I have been interested in translating some of their ideas into concrete. I like geometric rather than curvilinear forms, and I see the structure of the furniture pieces as sculpture, using angles to give them movement and direction.

I'm primarily a painter, but I've designed buildings, cars, and jewelry in addition to the furniture. All my ideas are interrelated. For example, when I was doing Minimal paintings and drawings, I used the angles of my chairs in large-scale drawings, and I expanded an idea for stacking chairs into a design for a high-rise. I'd have to say my furniture is as much my art as my painting is.

I always start with pure design, and whether it works or not is another story. I wanted to make sturdy chairs that would knock down so you could store them away or move them easily. I think these are very good solutions. I've also gone in the opposite direction from the plywood pieces, which are very transient in feeling, to working with concrete. The concrete tables are heavy and permanent. I don't know how to relate the two, but perhaps it's just that different people have been influences.

219. Alwy Visschedyk.
Concrete Clip Table.
1977.
Concrete, glass,
18 × 36 × 36".
Collection Mr. and Mrs. Ted Flicker,
Los Angeles

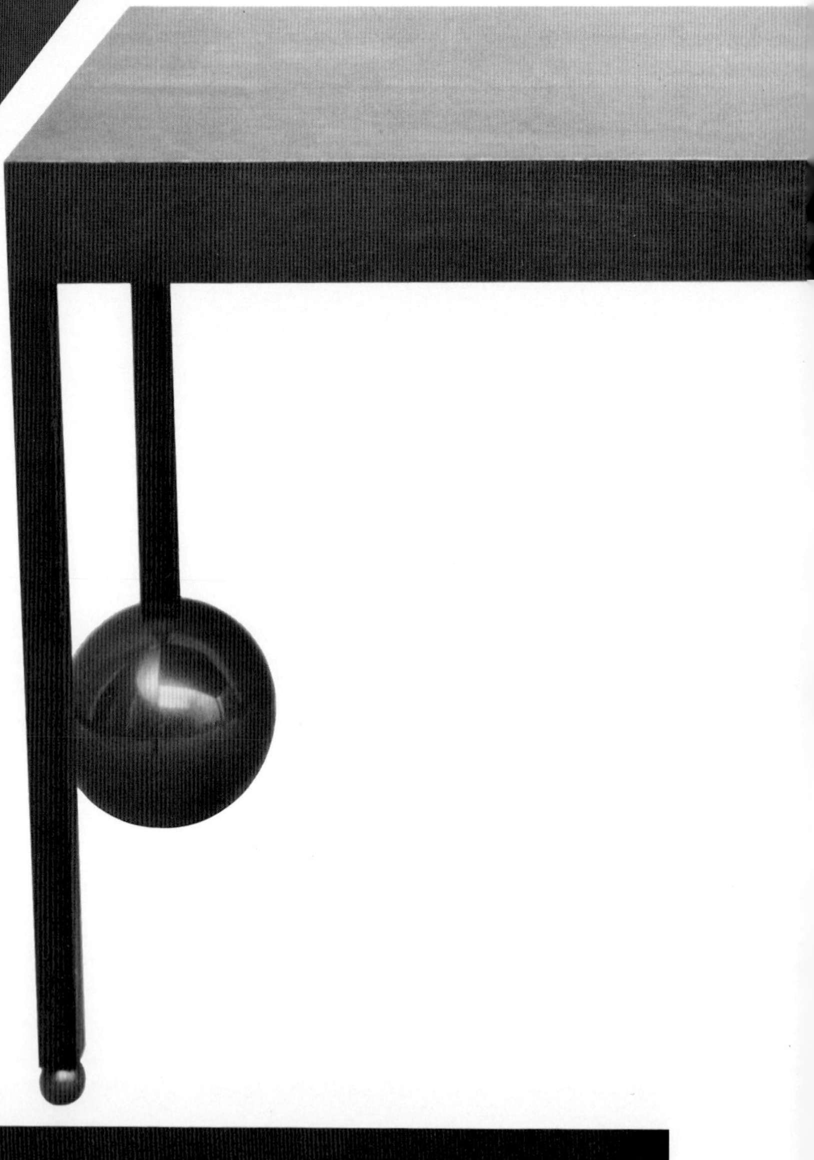

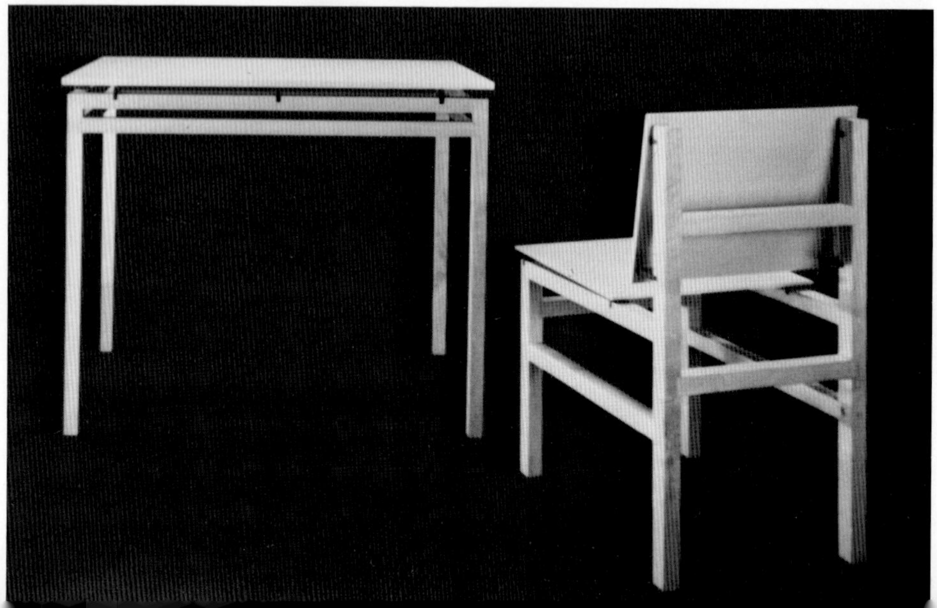

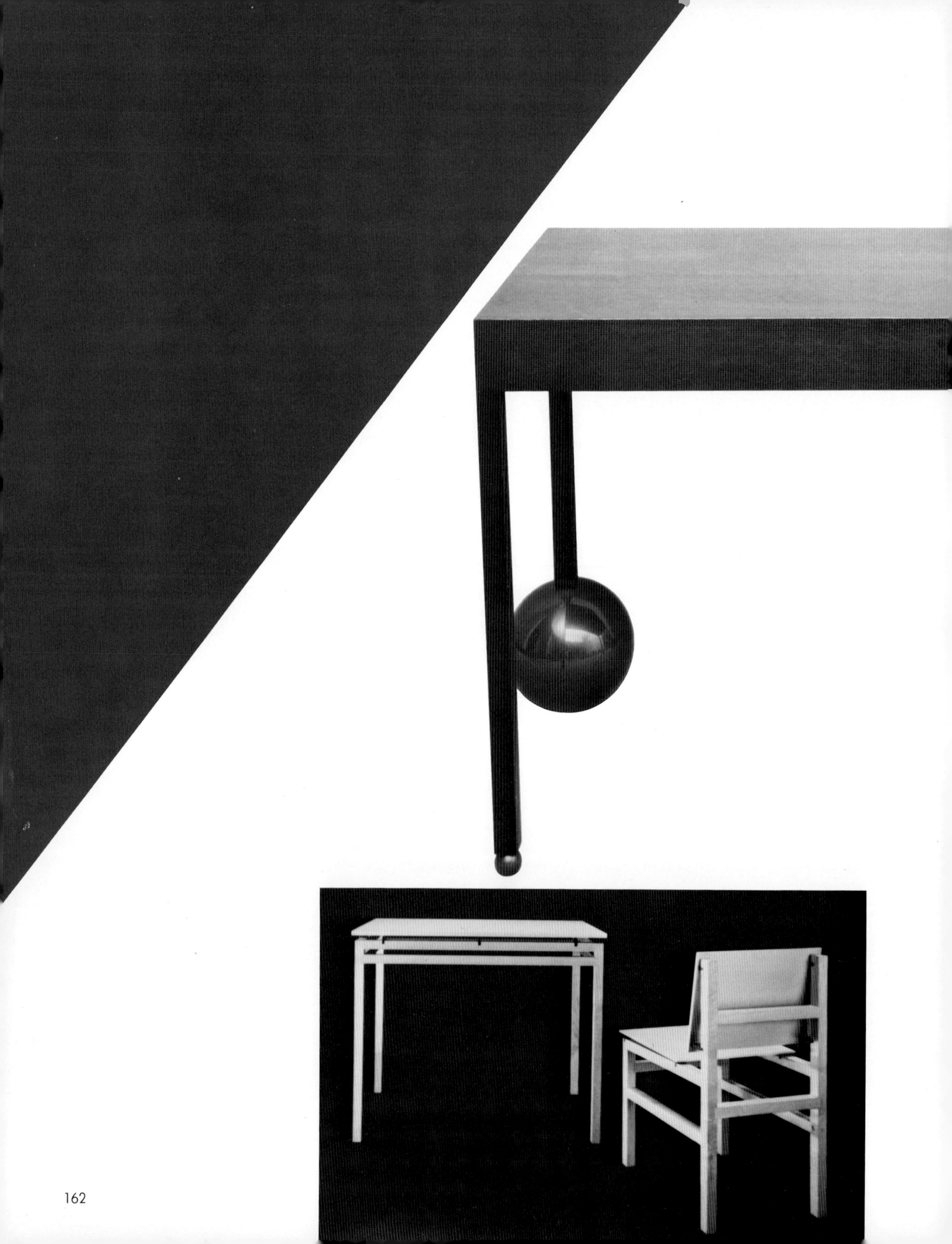

Robert Wilhite

Born in Santa Ana, California, 1946
Lives in Los Angeles

In the past I've done conceptual performances, made musical instruments, designed sets for theatrical performances, produced records, and made both paintings and sculptures. I've been making furniture since the mid-seventies. More recently I have expanded my concerns to other functional objects.

I believe good furniture can walk the delicate line between art and function. The problem is like balancing a four-sided scale of aesthetics, function, craftsmanship, and structure. I would say that with my work the scale favors aesthetics. I like simple geometric shapes, lines, and planes, and I also prefer asymmetry to symmetry. By using contrasting solid-colored hardwoods and lacquers, I can manipulate the lines and shapes in my furniture. I try to make all the elements in my work necessary to the structure, incorporating what might seem to be decorative into functional elements.

I am concerned with the craftsmanship in my work because I want the pieces to last. Furniture that is used on any regular basis takes a lot of abuse. If it isn't made well, it isn't going to last very long, and I believe a lack of craftsmanship is ultimately a distraction.

I've always felt that whether an object is art is a matter of aesthetic and conceptual recognition on the part of the viewer. I feel furniture is not necessarily a step down from sculpture because it does essentially the same thing, except that it functions as well.

220. Robert Wilhite.
Ball Table. 1982.
Stained walnut, lacquered wood,
29½ × 48 × 20".
Collection Mr. and Mrs. Jean Paul Coupel,
Caracas, Venezuela

221. Robert Wilhite. *Writing Table and Side Chair.* 1981.
Aluminum, ebony, maple, writing table: 29¾ × 30 × 24"; side chair: 32 × 18 × 24".
Collection the artist, Los Angeles

222. Robert Wilhite.
Diagonal Lamp. 1980.
Maple, ebony, aluminum, 72 × 18 × 23".
Collection Denise Domergue, Los Angeles

Robert Wilson

Born in Waco, Texas, 1941
Lives in New York

223. Robert Wilson. *Stalin Chairs*. 1977. Lead over fiberglass, 33×61×61". Collection Dr. Alvin F. Friedman-Kine, New York

I am an artist; my training is in architecture and painting. I also write plays and direct them. In architecture you study scale and proportion, time and space. In theater you deal with language, dance, philosophy, sculpture, architecture, painting—all the arts combined. Most playwrights are primarily concerned with the text, and frequently what you see is only illustrative background for what you're hearing.

[Continued]

224. Robert Wilson. *Queen Victoria Chairs*. 1977. Lead, brass, electric lights, 68½×47½×47½". Installation Contemporary Arts Center, Cincinnati, Ohio. Collection M. and Mme. Michel David-Weill

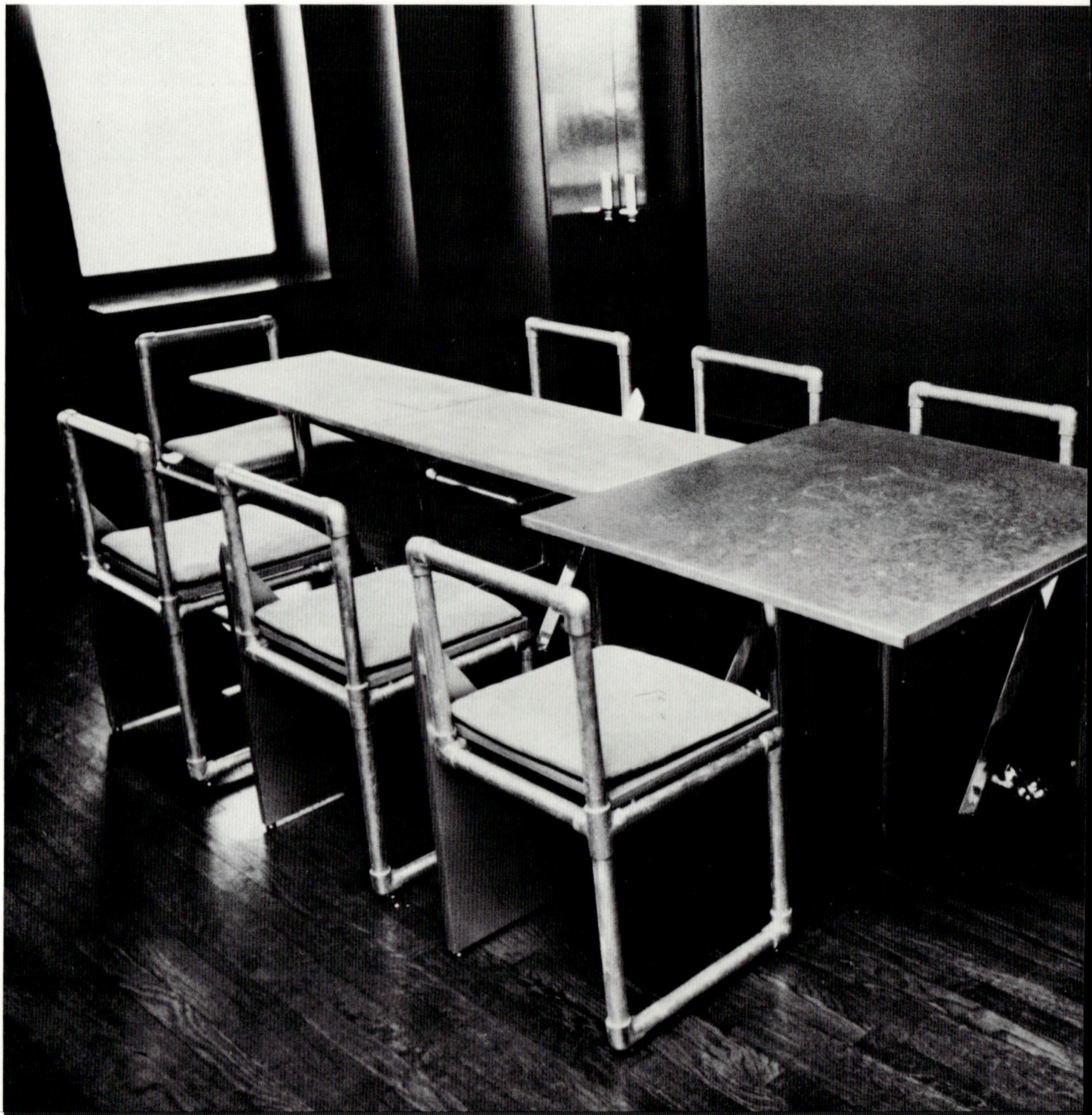

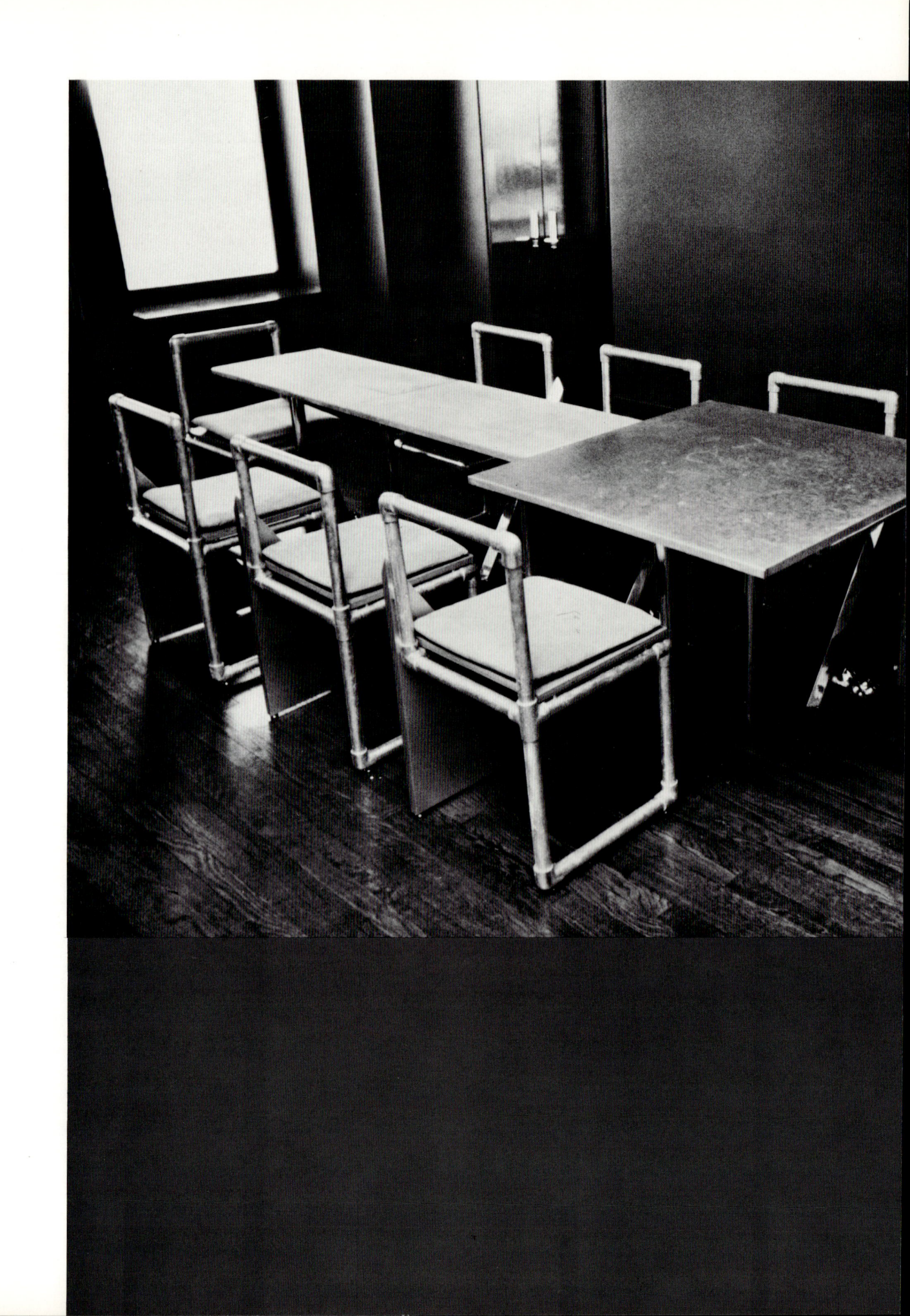

In my case I work slowly and meticulously with many sketches, diagrams, and mathematical equations to work out the structure, formal design, and movement of each part of a big play. Everything is separately conceived so each element can stand apart from its context. Then each part is put together in layers so the work is like a collage.

I have always had a fondness for furniture, and chairs have been the central image or sculptural element in my work. Sometimes people sit on them, sometimes they're just objects. The connotations change with respect to each play. I build small-scale and large-scale models, oversee their construction, and consider the minutest detailing. They can also function on their own as valid, independent works of art. In the plays, the chairs are lit as carefully as the actors. In fact sometimes you don't even see the actor, you see only the chair.

The *Dining Room Suite* was a commission. I came up with a concept of a flexible table that could seat a large number of people and one that could seat a small number of people. The basic table is twelve inches wide and twelve feet long, made out of galvanized sheet metal with chrome legs. It has three variable heights: fourteen inches off the ground, like a Japanese table, normal dining-room table height, and the height of a bar. It has four three-foot-square galvanized sheet metal leaves that can be added to the top as desired: all at once, just one, one at either end, and so forth. The small table seats four people comfortably. It is made out of dark green marble with a columnar mahogany base. The side chairs are made out of plumbing pipe with plywood seats. One side of the chair is supported by a brushed aluminum sheet with a gold cat's paw. The gray suede cushions are removable so one can use them to sit on the floor if the table is at the lowest height. Then I made a big armchair that is three-feet wide. It is made out of solid oak two-by-fours bolted together with big bolts. The concept was designed for that room, but the idea could be adapted anywhere.

225. Robert Wilson. *Dining Room Suite*. 1982. Mixed media. Collection Paul F. Walter, New York

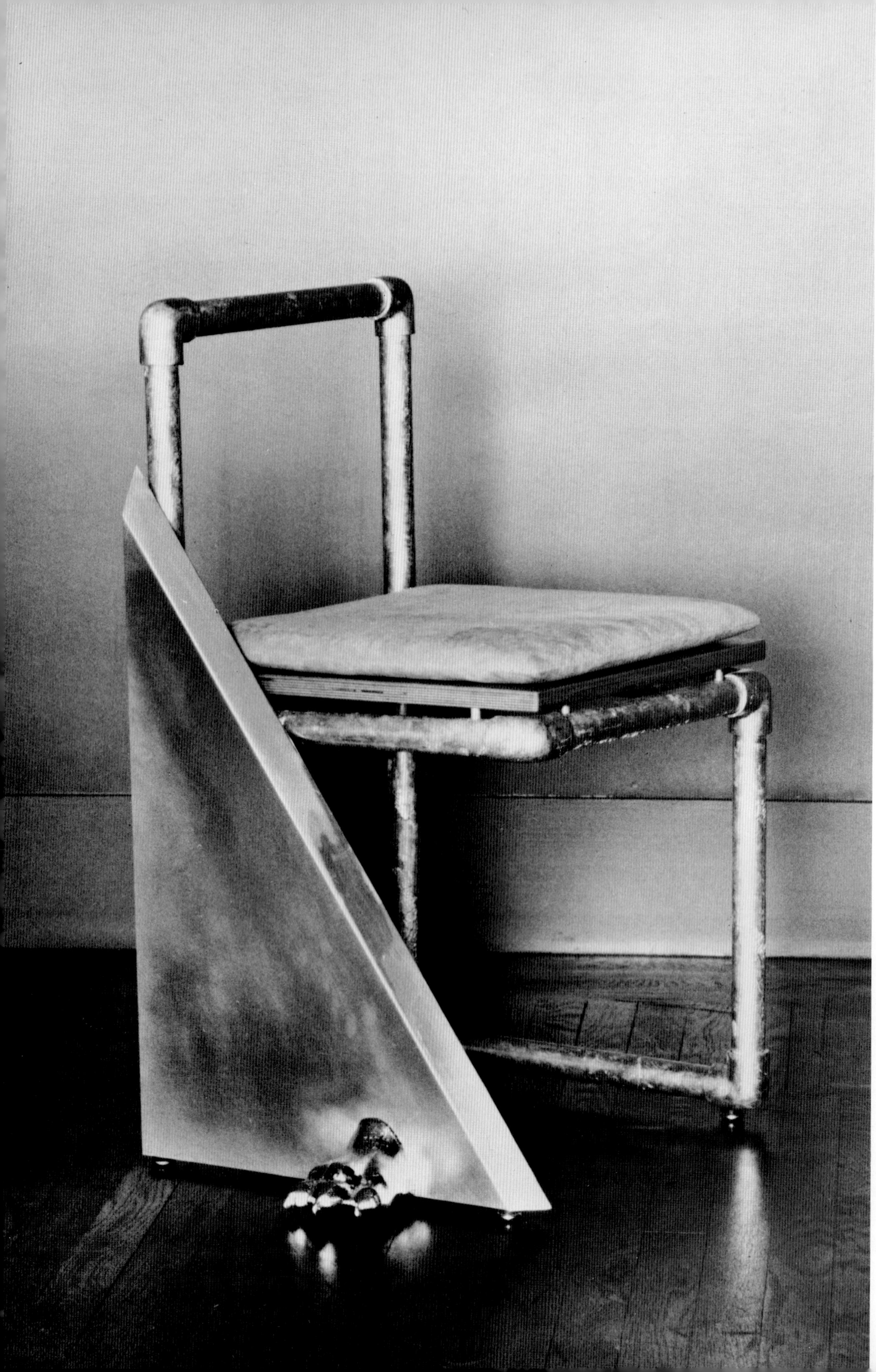

Opposite:
226. Robert Wilson. *Side Chair*. 1982.
Wood, plumbing pipe,
galvanized sheet metal, brass,
cushion, 32 × 16 × 16".
Collection Paul F. Walter, New York

227. Robert Wilson.
Beach Chairs. 1979.
Aluminum, 31 × 78 5/8 × 23 3/4";
22 × 78 5/8 × 23 3/4".
Installation Contemporary Arts Center, Cincinnati, Ohio.
Collection Schaubuhne am Halleschen Ufer

Jack Youngerman

Born in Louisville, Kentucky, 1926
Lives in New York

I'm interested in "art," period, rather than just "painting" or "sculpture." For example, Japanese culture recognizes that common objects can embody a quality that is a manifestation of the human spirit. I share the feeling that useful objects are not necessarily a lower form of expression. I like utilitarianism, and to me a Shaker chair is art. I wanted to get away from painting and literally bring it down to earth. The screen sits on the floor and isn't trying to be an icon. It is autonomous in that it is neither painting nor sculpture, doesn't demand a wall, and creates its own space. I made the first one in 1970; then in 1976 and 1978 I made some more.

My feeling is that categories in Western art are often arbitrary, artificial, and created for commercial reasons and intellectual convenience. I think that to a large degree Western ideas about art are derived from icons; there is that chapel spirit, where you set art apart and look at it humbly. I'm against aesthetic cults and object worship. They're almost idolatrous and have more to do with elitism and social orders than art.

Plainness and openness are my favorite aspects of American culture. The style, language, and taste I like come from the streets. It's the everyday, ordinary kind of activity that gives the basis for style and art. For me that is what the American spirit is all about and what I like about it. I have no talent as a craftsman and am involved in making works that are neither paintings nor sculptures as a matter of aesthetic necessity, but I do like the idea of people who make things. Actually everybody is capable of making something. I feel that to make anything as well as one can is a form of a meditative or votive act, and an act of respect for the whole human race.

228. Jack Youngerman. *Fire/Orange*. Folding screen, front and back. 1978. Oil and acrylic, raw linen, 72 × 144". Collection Cooper-Hewitt Museum, The Smithsonian Institution's National Museum of Design, New York

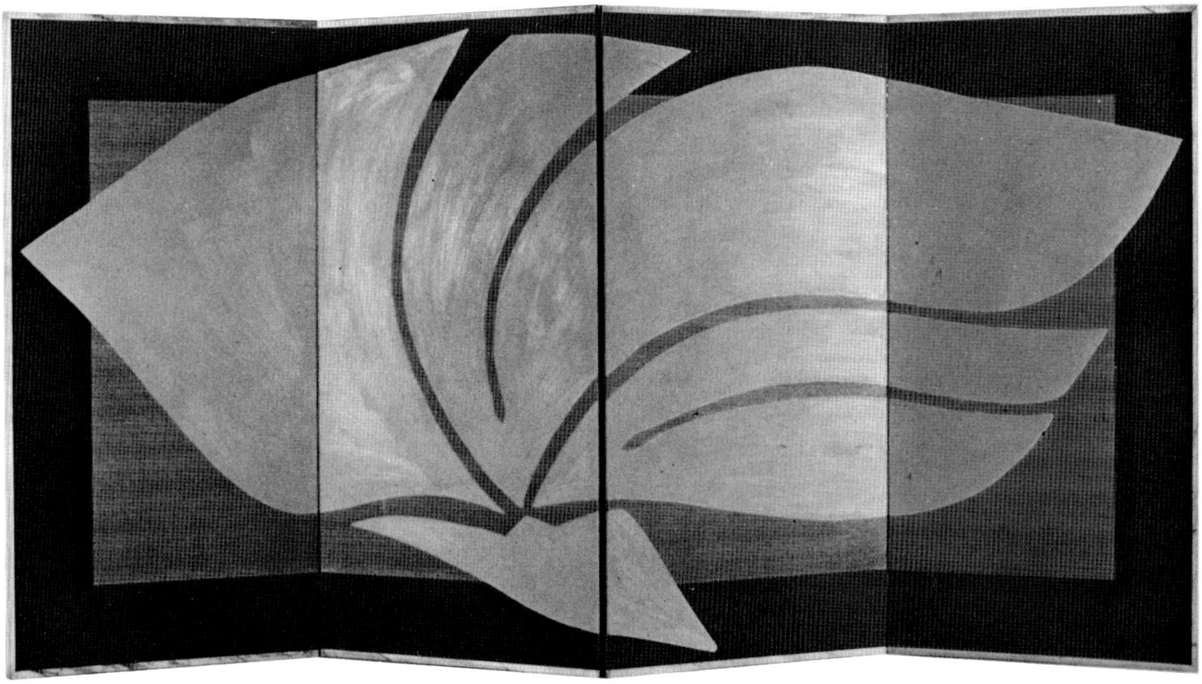

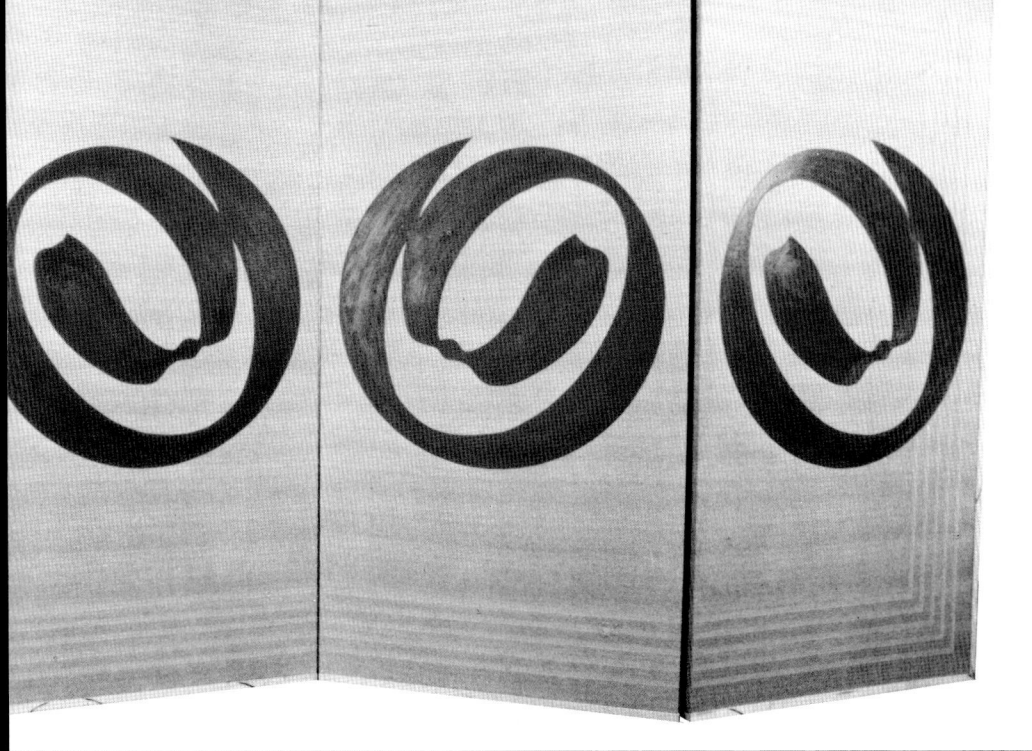

229. Jack Youngerman. *Two Blues*. Folding screen, front and back. 1978. Oil on linen, 72×144". Washburn Gallery, New York

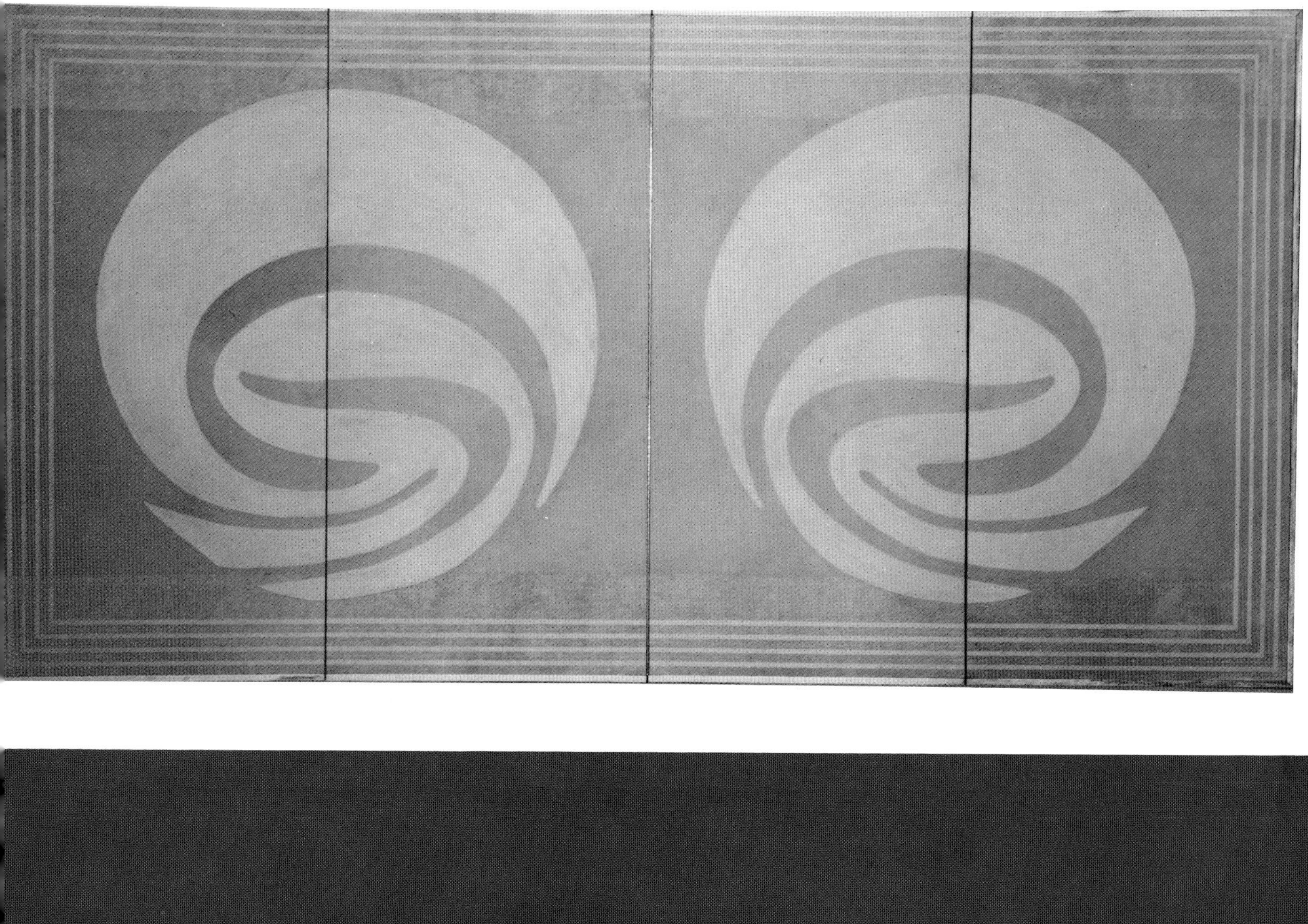

Acknowledgments

This project was a joy for me from start to finish, and this I owe to all who were involved in so many ways throughout its various stages. I would first like to express my heartfelt gratitude to all the artists with whom I corresponded and who sent me material whether or not they were included in the book. They gave me their precious time and allowed me the opportunity to sound them out. Their enthusiasm and cooperation inspired me to carry this project through. I would also like to thank the gallery personnel and the photographers who submitted material to make this book possible.

The single most instrumental person in the realization of this book was Olga Hammer, who took my idea seriously from the start and guided me through the process with her knowledge of how books are made, her organizational gifts, her moral support, and the months and months of cheerfully donated time and participation. I simply could not have done this without her.

I would also like to thank Leta Bostelman, managing editor at Harry N. Abrams, for her support and faith in me, as well as the rest of the helpful staff at Abrams, especially Anne Yarowsky and Carol Robson. Finally for their very special contributions, I thank Alan Abrams, Joseph Hammer, Tom Whitridge and Ink, Inc., Rick Kauffman, Tim Street-Porter, Rebecca Kamelhar, Jeff Book, John Chase, Janine Moss, and Nancy Reese.

Photograph Credits

Numbers refer to caption numbers

Michael Abramson, New York, 28
Michael Abramson, courtesy L. A. Louver Gallery, Venice, California, 1, 209, 210, 211
Clayton Adams, 162, 163, 164, 165
J. Gordon Adams, 74
The Albright Knox Gallery, Buffalo, New York, 51
Art et Industrie, New York, 72, 137, 169, 170, 171, 172
R. J. Bailie, Albuquerque, New Mexico, 24, 149
The Beinecke Library, Yale University, New Haven, Connecticut, 46
William H. Bengston, courtesy Phyllis Kind Gallery, New York, 34
Mary Bachmann, 204, 205, 206
Ferdinand Boesch, courtesy The Pace Gallery, New York, 35
Tad Bonsall, Pasadena, California, 98, 174, 219, 221, 222
Olivier de Bouchony, Paris, 13, 93
Fred J. Boyle, courtesy Nancy Hoffman Gallery, New York, 5, 11, 195, 196, 197, 198
Lee Brian, Palm Springs, California, 216
P. W. Brown, 95
Rudolph Burkhardt, courtesy Leo Castelli Gallery, New York, 7, 71
Gerry Cappel, 15
Gerry Cappel, courtesy Janus Gallery, Los Angeles, 14, 16, 191, 192, 193, 194
Centre Georges Pompidou, Paris, 47, 56, 57
Diana Church, 17, 125, 127, 128
Geoffrey Clements, courtesy Leo Castelli Gallery, New York, 99
Geoffrey Clements, courtesy Paula Cooper Gallery, New York, 30
Becky Cohen, courtesy Holly Solomon Gallery, New York, 2, 23, 152
Arch Connelly, New York, 90, 91
Cooper-Hewitt Museum, New York, 27, 228
James Dearing, New York, 140
D. James Dee, New York, 29
D. James Dee, courtesy Holly Solomon Gallery, New York, 146
Roy Elkind, 84
M. Lee Fatherlee, courtesy Leah Levy Gallery, San Francisco, 3, 130
Brian Forrest, 77, 78
Ron Forth, Cincinnati, Ohio, 224, 227
Roger Gass, courtesy Daniel Weinberg Gallery, Los Angeles/San Francisco, 22, 81, 82
Raenne Giavanni, 89, 118
Marian Goodman Gallery, New York, 115, 116, 117, 147, 223

Brian Hagiwara, 105
Bob Hanson, New York, 9, 143, 145
Bob Hanson, courtesy Julie: Artisan's Gallery, New York, 144
Glenn Heim, New York, 122
Byrd Hoffman Foundation, New York, 223, 224, 227
eeva-inkeri, New York, 184
eeva-inkeri, courtesy Holly Solomon Gallery, New York, 151
Dakota Jackson, Long Island City, New York, 132, 133
The Edward James Foundation, Sussex, England, 48
Jook, 158
Peter Kolk, 94
Randal Levenson, New York, 6, 225, 226
L. A. Louver Gallery, Venice, California, 123
Christopher Mann, 134, 135, 136
Bob Mates, New York, 26, 229
John Marshall, 167
Wendy Maruyama, Smithville, Tennessee, 161
Valentine Mayer, 124
Judy Kensley McKie, Cambridge, Massachusetts, 30, 168
David Mecey, 112
Alexander F. Milliken, Inc., New York, 86
Daniel Mularoni, New York, 201, 202, 203
The Museum of Contemporary Art, Caracas, Venezuela, 73
The Museum of Fine Arts, Boston, 166
The Museum of Modern Art, New York, 43, 52
Mike Narahara, 66, 67
Roger Nelson, 19, 25, 207, 208
The Norton Simon Museum, Pasadena, California, 37
The Oakland Museum, Oakland, California, 4, 97
Douglas Parker, courtesy Daniel Weinberg Gallery, Los Angeles/San Francisco, 83
James Patrick, courtesy Leo Castelli Gallery, New York, 185
Eric Pollitzer, Garden City, New York, 148
Bent Reij, 126
Karl H. Riek, Sebastopol, California, 96
Earl Ripling, 139
Laurel Ross, 173
Schopplein Studio, New York, 119, 120
Toby Seftel, New York, 175, 176, 177, 178, 179, 180, 181
Arlette Seligmann, New York, 49
Lori Seniuk, 16, 188, 189, 190
Frank Siciliano, New York, 153, 155, 156, 157
The Sidney Janis Gallery, New York, 33
Steven Sloman, New York, 79, 80, 85
George Steigelman, courtesy Leo Castelli Gallery, New York, 38, 68, 70, 186
Tim Street-Porter, Los Angeles, 21, 62, 63, 92, 113, 141, 142, 200
Kunie Sugiura, New York, 100, 101, 102, 182, 230
Soichi Sunami, courtesy The Museum of Modern Art, New York, 41, 60
The Tate Gallery, London, 44
Tecta-Mobel Manufacturers, West Germany, 54
Tim Thimmes, Los Angeles, 217, 218
John Thomson, Los Angeles, 12, 108, 109, 110, 111
Jerry L. Thompson, courtesy The Whitney Museum of American Art, New York, 36
Michael Todd, Los Angeles, 212, 213, 214
TTU Photo Service, 159, 160
Thomas P. Vinetz, Los Angeles, 20, 76, 138
Richard Walker, courtesy Leo Castelli Gallery, New York, 69
Dan Walworth, 32, 88
Kirk Winslow, p. 91, 131
Paul Yonge, 75
Zindman/Fremont, 121

230. Mark di Suvero. *Stool*. 1971.
Steel I-beam, 17¼ × 11¾ × 12".
Courtesy Oil & Steel Gallery, New York

Library of Congress Cataloging in Publication Data

Domergue, Denise.
　　Artists design furniture.

　　1. Furniture—Miscellanea.　I. Title.
TS885.D68　1984　　　684.1　　　83-21451
ISBN 0-8109-0932-4

Illustrations © 1984 Harry N. Abrams, Inc.
Excerpt from *A Sculptor's World* by Isamu Noguchi, 1968, reprinted by
permission of Harper & Row, Publishers, Inc.
Published in 1984 by Harry N. Abrams, Incorporated, New York
All rights reserved. No part of the contents of this book may be
reproduced without the written permission of the publishers

Printed and bound in Japan